PYTHON DATA SCIENCE FOR BEGINNERS

Unlock the Power of Data Science with Python and Start Your Journey as a Beginner (2023 Crash Course)

Rufus Johnston

Table of Contents

introduction

While thinking about how to build the kind of advanced society of the future, data is often mentioned as the most important idea to keep in mind. Several open-source IT environments are available to users today.

However, selecting the right tools and understanding how to use them can be difficult. The reality is that many different languages have been created, making it difficult for novices to choose the right one. Starting off just 25 years ago, Python has quickly risen to become a staple in beginning computer science courses at universities worldwide. Being proficient with Python for data analysis is crucial in the field of data science. Master the fundamentals, then go on to create amazing visuals.

Chapter 1:

A Short Introduction to Python

Learn the fundamentals of Python if you want to succeed in Data Science. Data Sciencester's orientation is mandatory for all new hires, and the highlight is a crash course on Python. This isn't meant to be a full Python tutorial. Instead, it will focus on the most important things.

Installing Python

Python may be downloaded at https://www.python.org/. To get the most recent version of Python for your OS, go over to the Downloads section.

The Zen of Python

These standards are based on those developed by Tim Peters. 20 guiding principles in The Zen of Python were used to create the Python programming language. Although it's not required that your Python code adheres to these standards, it is recommended that you do so. Remember that these recommendations are only suggestions that may be argued for or against; the Zen of Python is a hidden joke that surfaces if you run import this. They occasionally overlap to provide the most flexibility, as do all excellent moral rules.

Whitespace Formatting

Curly brackets are used to demarcate sections of code in most computer languages. Python, on the other hand, makes extensive use of indentation. This makes Python very readable. Unfortunately, formatting errors might completely ruin your work. Within parentheses and brackets, whitespace is ignored, which is helpful for complex computations.

Backslashes aren't used very often, but they can be used to show that a sentence goes on to the following line.

Whitespace formatting may make it more challenging to insert code into the Python shell. If you try to copy and paste the following code into the Python shell, for instance:

```
for i in [1, 2, 3, 4, 5]:
# notice the blank line
print i
```

Warning: The following problem has occurred:

Indentation Error: expected an indented block

This issue occurs because the interpreter thinks the for loop's block ends at the blank line.

IPython has a magical method called %paste that faithfully pastes the clipboard's contents, including any whitespace. And this is why IPython is so helpful.

Modules

Several Python features are hidden by default.Both built-in and add-on features, such as those from third-party developers, fall under this category. Putting these capabilities to use requires the import of the corresponding modules.

```python
import re
my_regex = re.compile("[0-9]+", re.I)
```

Here, re is the regular expressions module that contains the associated functions and constants. Following this import, calling those procedures without the re prefix is no longer possible .Use an alias instead of creating a new re in the code if you already have one.

This is still an option if the module's name is lengthy or you anticipate having to input it often. One such convention is:

```python
import matplotlib.pyplot as plt
```

Functions

A function is an instruction that takes in one or more arguments and returns the same number of results. It is the def keyword that is used to define functions in **Python**.

```python
def double(x):
    """this is where you put an optional docstring
    that explains what the function does.
    for example, this function multiplies its input by 2"""
    return x * 2
```

Python functions get treated as first-class citizens. That is, they may be stored in variables and sent to functions just like any other parameter. Furthermore, defining brief anonymous functions is a breeze:

```python
y = apply_to_one(Lambda x: x + 4) # equals 5
```

The def keyword is preferred over allocating lambdas to variables. You may use the default argument if you need to override the default value

for a function's parameters. In some instances, it's necessary to provide name arguments to provide more context.

Strings

Either single or double quotation marks may be used to specify a string.

> Num-1= "welcome"
>
> Num_2 = 'welcome'
>
> In Python, special characters are represented by using backslashes. For instance:
>
> tab_string = "\t"
>
> len(tab_string)
>
> Exceptions

Python is designed to "throw an exception" if anything goes wrong. If you don't handle these exceptions, your software will crash. Using try and accept to avoid unexpected program termination is thus essential.

```python
try:
print 0 / 0
except ZeroDivisionError:
print "cannot divide by zero"
```

Although exceptions aren't always applicable, they may help you write cleaner code in Python. The best Python programmers make it a practice to write exceptions.

Lists

In Python, a list is one of, if not the most, crucial data structures. When items are arranged in a particular order, we call it a list. Python lists have a lot in common with lists in other languages.

In Python, you may use the in operator to do a membership check on a list, as shown below:

```python
1 in [1, 2, 3] # True
0 in [1, 2, 3] # False
```

Joining lists together is a simple process:

```python
x = [1, 2, 3]
x.extend([4, 5, 6]) # x is now [1,2,3,4,5,6]
```

You can still use x if you don't want to change it, or you may use list addition instead.

```python
x = [1, 2, 3]
y = x + [4, 5, 6] # y is [1, 2, 3, 4, 5, 6]; x is unchange
```

Typically, you'll add items to lists one by one.If you know the maximum amount of items a list can hold, you can efficiently extract their contents. Nevertheless, a value Error will occur if the number of components on either side is different.

It's standard practice to use an underscore (_) to represent a null value:

```python
_, y = [1, 2] # now y == 2, didn't care about the first element
```

Dictionaries

One of Python's most powerful data structures is the dictionary (or hashtable). The good news is that you don't have to execute it manually since it's already embedded in the Python language.

A dictionary is an efficient data structure that stores information using the key and value pair. Each unique key in the dictionary corresponds to a specific value. Although the associated value need not be exceptional, it should be meaningful.

These are a few real-world applications of terms from the dictionary:

> The Subway Card You Use To Get Discounts
> A unique identifier for a college student.

A directory of telephone numbers
One that can be held in one's hands

Any kind of numeric or textual key may be used as the "key" within the dictionary. In fact, it may be any kind of information. The importance of the key's uniqueness cannot be overstated.

The Python programming language includes a dictionary as one of its many built-in data structures, making it an ideal learning environment for beginners. Moreover, we have access to a plethora of alternative data structures and methods. That might get downright frightening.

If you want to make a dictionary that behaves like a phone book, you'll have to decide whether the key will be a value or a name. A phone number may be used in the first scenario. As every phone number is

different, they make the perfect key. Even if remembering a person's number is more superficial, you may still use their name as a key.

```
phoneBook = {'Mike': 55555555} # 'Mike' is the key
```

You're limited to having just one buddy called "Mike" in this scenario. You'll have to keep track of any more Mikes as Mike01, Mike03, etc. However, here's an example of how to print only one phonebook entry:

'Mike' in the phone book

The print command may be used to show all of the information stored in the phonebook.

Over time, new words and phrases will need to be added to and added to the dictionary.

```
if 1 > 2:
message = "if only 1 were greater than two..."
elif 1 > 3:
message = "elif stands for 'else if'"
else:
message = "when all else fails use else (if you want to)"
```

A tertiary if-then-else on a single line is still possible and will be used on occasion:

```python
parity = "even" if x % 2 == 0 else "odd"
```

The while loop in Python allows you to:

```python
x = 0
while x < 10:
print x, "is less than 10"
x += 1
```

Although you'll often fill out applications for and in:

```python
for x in range(10):
print x, "is less than 10"
```

On the other hand, continue and break may be used if you need complicated logic.

Boolean

Python's Booleans function similarly to those of other languages, with one exception:

None indicates an empty value in Python. Comparable to the null of any other language:

Python's flexible Boolean support means you may use whatever value you choose in its place. These are several illustrations of the fallacy:

> None
> ""
>
> Set()
> 0
> 0.0
> None
> {} (an empty dict)

Generally, we accept as true any statement that is not explicitly false. With if reports, you can now look for things like empty lists, empty strings, etc. If you aren't prepared for this behavior, you may potentially encounter challenging issues.

A more straightforward approach to the same result is:

```
first_char = s and s[0]
```

When the first value is actual, the second is returned, and vice versa when the first is false. In addition to this, when x is an integer or None.
safe_x= x or 0

One may use any function in Python that returns True if and only if any item in the list is actual or all process, which does the same thing but returns True if at least one item in the list is accurate.

```
x = [4,1,2,3]
y = sorted(x) # is [1,2,3,4], x is unchanged
x.sort() # now x is [1,2,3,4]
```

The way the sort function works by default is to compare the items in a list and put them in order of decreasing size. You can tell the program to sort the items from largest to smallest by using the argument reverse = true. You can use a key instead of the things themselves to compare the result of a function you define.

List Comprehensions:
It's common to desire to transform one list into another by picking and choosing which items to include or exclude or by switching around the order of the items in the original list. Python's approach to this is to use list comprehensions:

```
even_numbers = [x for x in range(5) if x % 2 == 0] # [0, 2, 4]
squares = [x * x for x in range(5)] # [0, 1, 4, 9, 16]
even_squares = [x * x for x in even_numbers] # [0, 4, 16]
```

It is still possible to transform a list into a dictionary or set.
In cases when you don't want a specific value from the list, using an underscore (_) as the variable is acceptable.

Several terms may be included in a list of understanding if it includes:

```
pairs = [(x, y)
for x in range(10)
for y in range(10)] # 100 pairs (0,0) (0,1) ... (9,8), (9,9)
```

This means that the outcomes from earlier experiments may be used in subsequent experiments.

There will be several understanding applications in your future.
Generators and Iterators

One problem with lists is their potential for extreme size; a range of a million items, for instance, might result from the expression range (1000000). This may be relatively inefficient if you like to handle each one separately. It would be wasteful to calculate all of the numbers if you only needed the first handful.

Repeating a generator is possible because its values are created on demand.

A generator may be built with the help of functions and the yield operator:

```python
def lazy_range(n):
    """a lazy version of range"""
    i = 0
    while i < n:
        yield i
        i += 1
```

The loop above will take the supplied values one at a time until there are no more:

```python
for i in lazy_range(10):
    do_something_with(i)
```

Python 2's range is lazy, and the language itself contains a function called lazy range, or xrange. That is, it is possible to create an infinite series.
However, you shouldn't loop through it without some kind of break logic in place.

In contrast to being lazy, there are just so many times you can go over something. If you want to keep cycling over the same data, you need to either make a new generator or use a list.

Using comprehensions behind parentheses is another approach to constructing a generator.

The items () method is a vital part of dictionaries. When it is called, it returns a list of key-value pairs. The iteritems () method, which creates the key-value pairs slowly each time it is used, is the most common way to implement this pattern.

Randomness

Data science learners will often need to create random numbers and may do so using the random module.

```python
import random
four_uniform_randoms = [random.random() for _ in range(4)]
# [0.8444218515250481, # random.random() produces numbers
# 0.7579544029403025, # uniformly between 0 and 1
# 0.420571580830845, # it's the random
```

If you wish to get repeatable results, you should use the random module, which creates pseudorandom numbers based on an internal state you may define using the random—seed parameter.

When called with one or two parameters, random. randrange returns a random value from the given range ():

```python
random.randrange(10) # choose randomly from range(10) = [0, 1, ..., 9]
random.randrange(3, 6) # choose randomly from range(3, 6) = [3, 4, 5]
```

The following are some more approaches that may be of use to you. As an example, random .shuffle may be used to rearrange a list's items arbitrarily.

Using random. choice: function will randomly choose one item from a list.

```python
my_best_friend = random.choice(["Alice", "Bob", "Charlie"]) # "Bob" for me
```

Random. sample can also be used to pick a random subset of items without changing any of them.

You can call random. choice many times to choose a group of items with replacement:

```python
four_with_replacement = [random.choice(range(10))
for _ in range(4)]
# [9, 4, 4, 2]
```

Regular Expressions

The use of regular expressions allows for text searches. It's likely that they're informative and useful, but they're also so involved that they've inspired a library's worth of books. Here are some instances of how to use them in Python, and the few times we face them, you will learn more about them.

```python
import re

print all([ # all of these are true, because
not re.match("a", "cat"), # * 'cat' doesn't start with 'a'
re.search("a", "cat"), # * 'cat' has an 'a' in it
not re.search("c", "dog"), # * 'dog' doesn't have a 'c' in it
3 == len(re.split("[ab]", "carbs")), # * split on a or b to ['c','r','s']
"R-D-" == re.sub("[0-9]", "-", "R2D2") # * replace digits with dashes
]) # prints True
```

Object-oriented Programming

Classes may be defined in Python to encapsulate data and the operations performed on it. They may help streamline and simplify your code. It would be simpler to explain them by making a strongly annotated example.

For instance, you may need to create your own Set class in Python if you can't find one that suits your needs.

How should the group act as a whole? To manipulate a given Set instance, you may either add or delete elements or check to see whether the instance has a certain value. All of them will be generated as member functions, which you may access with a. following the Set object.

Functional Tools

Functions that are passed around may occasionally be used in part to construct other functions. Take the following two-variable function as an example.

```python
def exp(base, power):
    return base ** power
```

And you want to put it to use by creating a one-variable function called two to the, whose input is the result of the expression exp(power) and whose output is power (2, power)

You can do this with the def, of course, but it may become complicated:

```python
def two_to_the(power):
return exp(2, power)
```

Instead, you may use functools Partial:

```python
from functools import partial
two_to_the = partial(exp, 2) # is now a function of one variable
print two_to_the(3) # 8
```

You can still use partial applications to finish up later arguments as long as their names are given.

```python
square_of = partial(exp, power=2)
print square_of(3) # 9
```

If you can help it, you should avoid performing things like currying parameters within a function, where things quickly get confusing.

You might get the same results from a map, reduce, and filter as you would from a list comprehension.

```python
def double(x):
return 2 * x
xs = [1, 2, 3, 4]
twice_xs = [double(x) for x in xs] # [2, 4, 6, 8]
twice_xs = map(double, xs) # same as above
list_doubler = partial(map, double) # *function* that doubles a list
twice_xs = list_doubler(xs) # again [2, 4, 6, 8]
```

By making many lists, you may use a map that takes in an array of arguments.

In the same vein, the filter will do the job of list comprehension if:

```python
def is_even(x):
    """True if x is even, False if x is odd"""
    return x % 2 == 0
x_evens = [x for x in xs if is_even(x)] # [2, 4]
x_evens = filter(is_even, xs) # same as above
list_evener = partial(filter, is_even) # *function* that filters a list
x_evens = list_evener(xs) # again [2, 4]
```

And will combine the first two items in a list, then the next two, and so on, to produce a single output.

Enumerate

Sometimes it's useful to examine a list and use not just its items but also its indexes.

Enumerating produces tuples (index, element) and is typical of the Pythonic approach.

```python
for i, document in enumerate(documents):
    do_something(i, document)
```

To a similar extent, if you are solely interested in the indexes:

```python
for i in range(len(documents)): do_something(i) # not Pythonic
for i, _ in enumerate(documents): do_something(i) # Pythonic
```

Zip and Argument Unpacking

It is common practice to wish to compress many lists into one. Using Zip, you may combine many lists into one that has tuples of data that are paired together. The zip will instantly terminate when the first list expires if the lists have different lengths.

A list may be "unzipped," though, using a special trick:

```python
pairs = [('a', 1), ('b', 2), ('c', 3)]
letters, numbers = zip(*pairs)
```

For argument unpacking, the asterisk uses the members of pairs as separate arguments to zip. The call ends as though you had really made the call.

```python
zip(('a', 1), ('b', 2), ('c', 3))
```

The unpacking of arguments is applicable to any function:

```python
def add(a, b): return a + b
add(1, 2) # returns 3
add([1, 2]) # TypeError!
add(*[1, 2]) # returns 3
```

It's not often that something like this comes in useful, but when it does, it's a real game-changer.

Chapter 2:

Introduction to Data Science

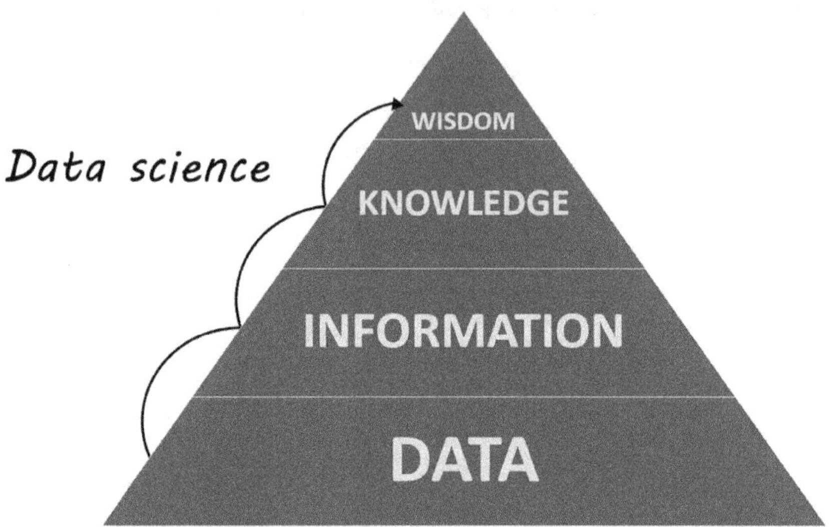

Data Science is a new branch of endeavor concerned with the collection, analysis, preparation, visualization, administration, and preservation of vast amounts of data. Although the term Data Science seems to be closely associated with subjects like databases and computer science, a variety of skills are necessary.

Some people associate Data Science with individuals clad in white lab coats sitting in front of computers. Yet this is not the case.
To begin, the vast majority of data on the planet is unstructured. To put it another way, the data is not structured in neat rows and columns. Think of a web page where friends share short comments and pictures, but there are only a few numbers to deal with. Even though schools, businesses, and governments probably use numbers, tax assessments and sales of products are two examples.

Nonetheless, statisticians examine a lot of information in the world. Hence, although strong arithmetic abilities are required, there is a lot to be done in the realm of data science for individuals who are comfortable dealing with sounds, words, photos, and other sorts of data.

Therefore, data science is more than simply data analysis. Many people like to study data and could spend all day looking at histograms and averages, but others would instead do something else. Data science has many uses and requires a wide range of skills. Let's learn more about this idea by looking at what you need to know to buy a box of cereal.

Whichever cereal you prefer—fibrous, nutty, or fruity—you prepare for the purchase by writing "cereal" on your shopping list. Your upcoming purchase is now a piece of data. When you go to the grocery store, you use that information as a reminder to grab your favorite item and place it in your basket. At the checkout, the clerk scans the barcode on your cereal box, and the price is entered into the cash register. Now, since you bought the last box in the store, a computer in the warehouse tells the stock manager that it's time to order more from the distributor. You also have a voucher for your box, which the clerk scans and gives you a specified discount. Near the end of the week, a report of all scanned manufacturer coupons is transmitted to the cereal business so that they may pay the grocery store for all of the coupon reductions they have given out to consumers. Finally, towards the end of the month, the shop manager gazes at the lovely collection of pie charts depicting all the various varieties of cereal that were sold.

Because of the high demand for fruity cereals, they intend to expand the store's restricted shelf space next month.

Thus, this little piece of information that began as a scribble on your shopping list ended up in a variety of locations, the most significant of which was on the manager's desk as a decision-making tool. The data traveled through many transformations on its way from your shopping list to the manager's desk. Except for the computers, where the data may have remained for some time, most pieces of hardware, such as the barcode scanner, were engaged in the data collection, transformation, and storage. Moreover, numerous types of software were used to organize, visualize, and display the data.

Finally, many "human systems" interacted with the data. Humans selected which systems to buy and install, who should have access to certain types of data, and what should happen to the data when its primary function was completed. Before the above scenarios happened, people at the supermarket chain and its partners had to make careful decisions and negotiate.

Data scientists do not take part in all of these procedures.
They do not create computers or barcode scanners. So, where do data scientists play the most important role? Data scientists, in general, play the most active roles in the following fields: data collection, data archiving, data analysis, and data architecture.

Let's look at them one by one, using cereal as an example. When designing the "point of sale" system's architecture, it was important to think about how different people would use the system's data. For example, the design of the system takes into account that both the stock manager and the shop manager might need access to the information scanned at the register for different reasons. A data scientist would support the system architect by providing feedback on how the data should be routed and arranged in order to improve data analysis, presentation, and visualization to the appropriate employees.

After that, data collection is about how data are gathered and shown before they are analyzed and presented. For example, each barcode indicates a number that is unrelated to the product it represents. Several barcodes are used to identify the same product. When should you add a little note stating that purchases X and Y are the same product, only in different packages?

Before data can be analyzed in a useful way, it needs to be represented, categorized, converted and linked. The data scientist is responsible for all of these steps.

Data scientists are heavily engaged in the analysis step.

In this example, you'll use analysis to summarize data, samples to infer larger contexts, and data visualization to highlight it in tables and even animations. Even though these tasks involve a lot of math, technology, and statistics, keep in mind that the end goal of data analysis is to help people. These are the "users" of the data. As a result, the most important task of a data scientist is to meet their demands.

This concept emphasizes the need for excellent communication abilities in data science. Even the most advanced statistical analysis will be useless if the results can't be explained to the person who needs them.

Ultimately, the data scientist must take part in data archiving. The preservation of acquired data in a way that makes it reusable—what you may call "data curation"—is a hard challenge since it is impossible to forecast all of the data's future uses. For example, when Twitter engineers were working on how to store tweets, they probably didn't anticipate tweets to be used to highlight earthquakes and tsunamis, but they had enough data to recognize that "geocodes" data reveals the geographical location from where a tweet was received.

After all, the cereal box and grocery store examples demonstrate where data scientists should continue to work and the abilities they need. The following are the abilities highlighted in the example:

Interact with data users-A data scientist should have solid communication skills in order to understand user preferences. It takes a lot of ability to translate between statistical scientific words and application domain jargon.
Understanding the application domain. The data scientist must rapidly learn how to use data in a given setting.

Visualizing a complex system's overall picture. After the data scientist learns about the application domain, he or she must think about how the data will be shared among all the important systems and people.

Recognize how data may be expressed. It is critical for data scientists to understand how data is stored and linked.

Transformation and analysis of data. Once data is in the hands of decision-makers, data scientists must understand how to modify, summarize, and draw conclusions from it. As was already said, it's important to know how to explain the results of an analysis to consumers.

Quality is prioritized. There is no such thing as flawless data, no matter how wonderful it is. It is your responsibility as a data scientist to understand the constraints of the data you deal with, to understand how you will assess its correctness, and to be able to offer strategies to improve data quality in the future years.
Moral reasoning. If data is important enough to gather, it must have an influence on people's lives. So, data scientists need to know about important ethical issues like security and be able to work with data constraints to stop data abuse.

The talents and abilities listed above are only the tips of the iceberg, but they demonstrate what a diverse spectrum is covered here. Einstein uploading up to get together with. The data scientist should be very good at thinking about systems and be able to think critically about how data will be used to make decisions that will affect people's lives. Of course, there are a few individuals that excel at these things, so some who are interested in data will specialize in one area, while others will specialize in another. This highlights the need for collaboration.
Many data challenges of varying complexity will be utilized in this introduction to Data Science to illustrate the skills and talents needed by data scientists.

Exploring Data Problems

Data science is distinct from other disciplines, such as statistics and mathematics. Data science is an applied process that data scientists use to meet the needs of data consumers and solve their problems. Before you can discover a solution to an issue, you must first recognize it, which is not as simple as it may look. This section will look at how to identify data issues.

Apple growers are terrified of their flowers and, eventually, their fruit. A frost in late April might ruin the flowers. In the summer, strong winds or hail may kill the fruit. In general, farming is a job that is often affected by the way the world looks.

Is there room for data science in today's physical world of unpredictable natural forces? There is, of course. So how can you be sure? To have a tip for finding data problems, you need to be open, creative, curious, and willing to ask a lot of questions. In fact, removing the concept that data scientists sit in front of a computer all day and use wacky software like Python is a mistake. Each data scientist must be satisfied with the issue area in which she works. Although the data scientist may never become a farmer, if you want to find data issues that farmers face, you must put yourself in their shoes. To put it another way, you must learn to think like a farmer on some level.

You may choose to read or watch videos to get this domain expertise, but the best option is to question "subject matter specialists" about what they do. The whole act of asking questions deserves its own treatment, but for now, there are three things to keep in mind while doing so. Initially, you'll need subject matter experts to tell tales about what they do. Then you want to ask them about anomalies, which are unusual occurrences that happen for better or worse. Lastly, it would help if you understood risks and uncertainty. In what kinds of situations is it hard to know what will happen next, and what happens next may have a big impact on whether the situation ends well or badly? Each of the following fields of study has a way to find problems with data that can be fixed by using data, knowledge, and making the right choice at the right time.

The rationale for asking for tales is that people think in terms of stories. Everyone knows and tells tales about their successes and failures in their own fields, from farmers to CEOs. Tales are important techniques of disseminating knowledge among people of the same profession, as well as methods of establishing a feeling of identity that distinguishes one profession from another. The only difficulty is that tales might be fake.

You can then look into how to back up these stories if you can get an expert to tell you the main stories that show how she does her job. Without questioning the truth of the tale's narrator, you might investigate techniques of assessing the many elements of how things happen in the narrative with an emphasis on validating the stories that guide professional activity.

Another way to find a problem is to look for both good and bad situations that are out of the ordinary. Highlighting abnormal situations is a terrific method to understand how things function, but in order to have an accurate picture of what initiates an abnormal case, it's vital first to describe the most typical occurrences.

A strong wind blew across the orchard as we returned to our farmer friend, causing the fruits to tumble off the trees. The majority of the plants lost some fruit. The fruits that had fallen could be seen at the tree's base. Another small cluster of trees looked to lose a lot of fruit, and the drops were usually distributed farther away from the trees. Is it feasible that unusual wind conditions exacerbated the problem in this specific location? Is it a coincidence that a few trees in the same place shed more fruit than usual?

A systematic count of lost fruit under a random sample of trees might aid in answering this issue. The majority of the succeeding trees would have lost the same amount, but more crucially, that "typical" group would provide a standard against which we could assess what was really odd.

When you uncover a series of situations that are out of the ordinary, you might focus your attention on them to attempt to comprehend the oddity.

Determine the risk and uncertainty as a third technique for defining data challenges. The primary role of information is to reduce uncertainty. Because of the way risk influences what you do, it is always necessary to reduce ambiguity. Life is full of dangers at home, school, and work. Deciding or failing to make a choice sets in motion a series of circumstances that may or may not be favorable. It's difficult to tell, but in general, you want to limit things down in a manner that minimizes the likelihood of a terrible one. To do this, you must make helpful judgments, and better decisions must reduce ambiguity. A data scientist may focus on the topics that matter by asking questions about risks and uncertainties. You may also use the previous two strategies—asking about tales that need professional knowledge and about anomalies.

Chapter 3:

Raw Data

In the world of Data Science, raw data comes in a variety of shapes and sizes. Generally, many other sorts of information may be extracted from this raw data. Amazon, for example, keeps a record of every user's click stream data on the website. This data can be used to figure out if a user is price-conscious or likes to buy popular items. You must have seen Amazon's suggested items. Some goods are created using such data.

Parsing raw data is the first step in the analytical process. The following phases are involved in data parsing:

Extraction of data from the source. Einsteiner uploaded with. Python uses necessary libraries to simplify the data from various sources.

Cleaning up data. After making sure the data is correct, please clean it up well so it can be used best for analysis. You could have a dataset with information on a class's pupils' weight, height, and grades. There may also be rows where the height is missing. Depending on the results of the study, these rows with missing data may be thrown out or replaced with the average weight or size.

Arrays with NumPy
Python has a data structure, such as a List, that can be optimized for array operations by default; however, a Python list on its own isn't ideal for performing sophisticated mathematical operations.

NumPy is a fantastic Python library created by Travis Oliphant that was designed primarily for scientific uses. It can cope with big matrices and has a vast library of high-level mathematical functions.

A NumPy array would use significantly less memory to hold the same amount of data as a Python list, allowing for faster reading and writing from the array.

Building an Array
To make a NumPy array object, you can give the next array function a group of integers:

```
>>> import numpy as np
>>> n_array = np.array([[0, 1, 2, 3],
[4, 5, 6, 7],
[8, 9, 10, 11]])
```

A NumPy array object has a lot of properties that help with how the information in the array is shown. These are some of its characteristics:

Ndim: This indicates how many dimensions the array has. For example,

```
>>>n_array.ndim
2
```

The shape of the array represents the size of each dimension:

```
>>>n_array.shape
(3,4)
```

The first dimension of the n array is 3 in size, while the second dimension is 4 in size. This is represented by three rows and four columns.

Size. This displays how many components there are:

>>>n_array.size

12

The total number of entries in the n array is 12.

Dtype: This indicates the data type of the array's elements:

>>> n_array.dtype.name

Int64

Mathematical Operations

You may wish to do certain mathematical operations on an array of data. This section will go through a few important ones.

Array Subtraction

The c array is obtained by subtracting an array from the b array. The subtraction is carried out element by element.Please keep in mind that when subtracting two arrays, they must be of identical size.

Squaring an Array

This command multiplies each element by two to get the following result:

>>> b**2

[1 4 9 16]

A Trigonometric Function Conducted on the Array

This command applies cosine to each value in the b array to get the following result:

```
>>> np.cos(b)
[ 0.54030231 -0.41614684 -0.9899925 -0.65364362]
```

Conditional Operations

To create the needed Boolean values, the conditional command performs a conditional operation on each member of the b array:

>>> b<2

[True False False False]

Matrix Multiplication

A dot product may be used to multiply two matrices element by element. The following instructions will test element-by-element multiplication:
>>> A1 = np.array([[1, 1],
[0, 1]])
>>> A2 = np.array([[2, 0],
[3, 4]])
>>> A1 * A2
[[2 0]
[0 4]]
The dot product can be computed using the following
command:
>>>np.dot(A1, A2)
[[5 4]
[3 4]]

Indexing and Slicing
If you want to choose a certain array element, you may do it by using indexes:
>>>n_array[1, 2]

This will choose the second array, followed by the third array value. It may alternatively be thought of as the intersection of the matrix's first row and second column.If you need to highlight a range of numbers in a row, use the following command:

```
>>> n_array[ 0 , 0:3 ]
[0 1 2]
```

The first three numbers in the first row are represented by the 0.3 value. The following command will highlight the full row of values:
>>>n_array[0 , :]
[0 1 2 3]
By using this command, the whole column of values require to beselected:
>>>n_array[: , 1]
[1 5 9]

Shape Modification

When the array is constructed, it has the ability to modify its shape. The following command flattens the array.

>>>n_array.ravel()

[0 1 2 3 4 5 6 7 8 9 10 11

The preceding command alters the array's shape to six rows and two columns. Remember that when reshaping, the new form should have the same number of components as the original:

```
>>> n_array.shape = (6,2)
>>> n_array
[[ 0  1]
 [ 2  3]
 [ 4  5]
 [ 6  7]
 [ 8  9]
 [10 11]]
```

The array shown above may be transposed to become:

```
>>> n_array.transpose()
[[ 0  2  4  6  8 10]
 [ 1  3  5  7  9 11]]
```

Authorizing Data Analysis Using Pandas

Pandas is a free and open-source library. The library is intended only for data analysis. Pandas is based on NumPy, making it simple to deal with data.

The Panda library offers efficient data structures for processing data, performing rapid joins, and reading data from many sources.

The Data Structure of Pandas

The Panda's library consists mostly of three data structures:

    Panel

    Series

    DataFrame

Series

A series is a one-dimensional array that may hold any sort of data, including floats, texts, integers, and Python objects. The following routines may be used to construct a series:

```
>>> import pandas as pd
>>> pd.Series(np.random.randn(5))
0  0.733810
1 -1.274658
2 -1.602298
3  0.460944
4 -0.632756
dtype: float64
```

The series index may be customized by using the functions listed below:

```
>>> pd.Series(np.random.randn(5), index=['a', 'b', 'c', 'd', 'e'])
a -0.929494
b -0.571423
c -1.197866
d  0.081107
e -0.035091
dtype: float64
A series can be derived from a Python dict too:
>>> d = {'A': 10, 'B': 20, 'C': 30}
>>> pd.Series(d)
A 10
B 20
C 30
dtype: int64
```

DataFrame

The DataFrame is a 2D data structure that contains columns of several data kinds. This may be interpreted as a table. The following data structures may be combined to form a DataFrame:

An array in NumPy

A NumPy 2D array

Dicts

Lists

When you write the following instructions, you may construct a DataFrame from a dict of series:

```
>>> d = {'c1': pd.Series(['A', 'B', 'C']),
'c2': pd.Series([1, 2., 3., 4.])}
>>> df = pd.DataFrame(d)
>>> df
c1 c2
0 A 1
1 B 2
2 C 3
3 NaN 4
```

Panel

A Panel is a data structure that handles 3D data. The following command shows an example of a panel:

```
>>> d = {'Item1': pd.DataFrame(np.random.randn(4, 3)),
'Item2': pd.DataFrame(np.random.randn(4, 2))}
>>> pd.Panel(d)
<class 'pandas.core.panel.Panel'>
Dimensions: 2 (items) x 4 (major_axis) x 3 (minor_axis)
Items axis: Item1 to Item2
Major_axis axis: 0 to 3
Minor_axis axis: 0 to 2
```

According to the preceding instructions, there are two DataFrames represented by two items. There are four rows, each with four great axes and three columns, each with three minor axes.

Inserting and Exporting Data

The data is stored in several formats, including databases, CSV, tsv, and so on. The Panda library allows you to read data from these formats and export it to the following formats. You'll be working with a dataset that contains the weight statistics of the children at the US school.

You'll use the following file structure:

Column	Description
LOCATION CODE	Unique location code
COUNTY	The county the school belongs to
AREA NAME	The district the school belongs to
REGION	The region the school belongs to
SCHOOL YEARS	The school year the data is addressing
NO. OVERWEIGHT	The number of overweight students
PCT OVERWEIGHT	The percentage of overweight students
NO. OBESE	The number of obese students
PCT OBESE	The percentage of obese students
NO. OVERWEIGHT OR OBESE	The number of students who are overweight or obese
PCT OVERWEIGHT OR OBESE	The percentage of students who are overweight or obese
GRADE LEVEL	Whether they belong to elementary or high school
AREA TYPE	The type of area
STREET ADDRESS	The address of the school
CITY	The city the school belongs to
STATE	The state the school belongs to
ZIP CODE	The zip code of the school
Location 1	The address with longitude and latitude

CSV

Enter the read csv function to read data from a.csv file:

```
>>> d = pd.read_csv('Data/Student_Weight_Status_Category_Reporting_Results__Beginning_2010.csv')
>>> d[0:5]['AREA NAME']
```

To enter data, the read csv method takes the path to the.csv file. After this, the program outputs the first five rows of the Location column in the data.

The t0 csv function may be used to write data to the.csv file.

```
>>> d = {'c1': pd.Series(['A', 'B', 'C']),
'c2': pd.Series([1, 2., 3., 4.])}
>>> df = pd.DataFrame(d)
>>> df.to_csv('sample_data.csv')
```

With the to csv method, the DataFrame is written to a.csv file. The location and filename where the file is to be built should be specified.

XLS

In order for pandas to read data from an Excel file, the xlrd package, in addition to the pandas package, must be installed.

The previous function is similar to the CSV reading command. The xlwt package must be installed in order to write to an Excel file.
>>>df.to_excel('sample_data.xls')
JSON
Python's standard JSON library may be used to read data from a JSON file. The commands listed below may help you read the file.

```
>>> import json
>>> json_data = open('Data/Student_Weight_Status_Category_Reporting_Results__Beginning_2010.json')
>>> data = json.load(json_data)
>>> json_data.close()
```

The open() function in the preceding command establishes a connection to the file. The data is loaded into Python using the JSON.load () method. The jsondata.close() method ends the file connection.
Panda's library also provides a function to read the JSON file, which may be accessed through the pd.readjson method ().

Database
Use the following function to get data from a database:
>>>pd.read_sql_table(table_name, con)

The preceding command generates a . If a table name and an SQLAlchemy engine are supplied, they will yield a . The DBAPI connection is not supported by this function. The aforementioned characteristics are described in detail below.

Table name. It refers to the name of the SQL table inside a database, as the name implies.
Con: This term refers to the SQLAlchemy engine.
The following program reads a SQL query into a DataFrame:
>>>pd.read_sql_query(sql, con)
The following are the parameters that were used:
Sql. einsteineruploading up to get together with.
Con. This is the SQLAlchemy engine.

Cleansing of Data

Data in row form requires cleaning before it can be evaluated or used to generate a dashboard. There are several things that might cause data difficulties. For example, a retail store's POS system may have malfunctioned and entered certain data with missing values. This section will show you how to deal with such information.

Search for Missing Data

Most data will have missing values in general. There might be many explanations for this, including the fact that the values were not gathered by the source system or that the values never existed. After the data has been imported, it is critical to look for missing characteristics in the data. The missing data must be handled in accordance with the standards. It may be fixed by removing a row or substituting a missing value with an alternate value.

In the instance of the Student Weight data, you may use the following command to see whether the location column has a missing value:

```
>>> d['Location 1'].isnull()
```

The not null () method returns True or False for each row of the value. If it is false, there is a missing value. This information may be combined to determine the number of missing value instances:

```
>>> d['Location 1'].isnull().value_counts()
```

The accompanying command demonstrates that the Location 1 column has 24 missing data. These missing values may be filled in by eliminating the rows with missing values or replacing them with other values. Use the following command to remove the rows:

```
>>> d = d['Location 1'].dropna()
```

The following command may be used to delete all the rows that have an instance of missing values:

```
>>> d = d.dropna(how='any')
```

Complete the Missing Data

Let's create some s to work with:

```
>>> df = pd.DataFrame(np.random.randn(5, 3), index=['a0', 'a10',
'a20', 'a30', 'a40'],
columns=['X', 'Y', 'Z'])
>>> df

X Y Z
a0 -0.854269 0.117540 1.515373
a10 -0.483923 -0.379934 0.484155
a20 -0.038317 0.196770 -0.564176
a30 0.752686 1.329661 -0.056649
a40 -1.383379 0.632615 1.274481
```

Add some more row indexes to produce null values inside the

:

```
>>> df2 = df2.reindex(['a0', 'a1', 'a10', 'a11', 'a20', 'a21',
'a30', 'a31', 'a40', 'a41'])

>>> df2
X Y Z
a0 -1.193371 0.912654 -0.780461
a1 NaN NaN NaN
a10 1.413044 0.615997 0.947334
a11 NaN NaN NaN
a20 1.583516 1.388921 0.458771
a21 NaN NaN NaN
a30 0.479579 1.427625 1.407924
a31 NaN NaN NaN
a40 0.455510 -0.880937 1.375555
a41 NaN NaN NaN
```

If you want to replace the null values in the df2 DataFrame with zero
values, use the following command:

```
>>> df2.fillna(0)
      X        Y         Z
a0 -1.193371 0.912654 -0.780461

a1 0.000000 0.000000 0.000000
a10 1.413044 0.615997 0.947334
a11 0.000000 0.000000 0.000000
a20 1.583516 1.388921 0.458771
a21 0.000000 0.000000 0.000000
a30 0.479579 1.427625 1.407924
a31 0.000000 0.000000 0.000000
a40 0.455510 -0.880937 1.375555
a41 0.000000 0.000000 0.000000
```

String Operations

You may wish to modify the string field column in your data from time to time. Here's a method for describing certain string operations:

Substring: To begin, choose the first five rows of the data's AREA NAME column as the sample data to change.

```
>>> df = pd.read_csv('Data/Student_Weight_Status_Category_Reporting_Results__Beginning_2010.csv')
>>> df['AREA NAME'][0:5]
```

To extract the first word from the Area Name column, use the extract function as shown in the command below:

```
>>> df['AREA NAME'][0:5].str.extract('(\w+)')
```

The str characteristic of the series is used in the preceding command. The str class provides a sophisticated extract function that accepts a common expression to extract data. The second word in AREA NAME may also be retrieved as a distinct column:

```
>>> df['AREA NAME'][0:5].str.extract('(\w+)\s(\w+)')
```

To mine data from several columns, the necessary regular expressions should be separated by parenthesis.

Filtering: If you wish to filter rows based on ELEMENTARY school data, use the following command:

```
>>> df[df['GRADE LEVEL'] == 'ELEMENTARY']
```

Uppercase: To modify the region name to uppercase, enter the command:

```
>>> df['AREA NAME'][0:5].str.upper()
```

There will be no noticeable difference since the data strings are already in uppercase.

Lowercase: To convert the Area Name to lowercase, use the following command:

```
>>> df['AREA NAME'][0:5].str.lower()
```

Length. You will use the following command to calculate the length of each element in the Region Name column:

```
>>> df['AREA NAME'][0:5].str.len()
0  47
1  47
2  47
3  27
4  27
Name: AREA NAME, dtype: int64
```

Split: Use the following command to split Area Name based on whitespace:

```
>>> df['AREA NAME'][0:5].str.split(' ')
```

Replace: If you wish to change all area names that end in DISTRICT to DIST, run the following command:

```
>>> df['AREA NAME'][0:5].str.replace('DISTRICT$', 'DIST')
```

The regular expression to be used to highlight the area of the text to replace is represented by the first parameter in the replacement function. The value to be substituted is represented by the second argument.

Merging Data

The pandas concat function may be used to aggregate data collections. Examine the Area Name and Country columns, which appear in the first five rows:

```
>>> d[['AREA NAME', 'COUNTY']][0:5]
```

You may still split the data as shown below:

```
>>> p1 = d[['AREA NAME', 'COUNTY']][0:2]
>>> p2 = d[['AREA NAME', 'COUNTY']][2:5]
```

p1 contains the first two rows of data, while p2 contains the last three rows. The concat() method may be used to join these pieces together. For example:

>>>pd.concat([p1,p2])

By designating a key, the combined pieces may be identified:

```
>>> concatenated = pd.concat([p1,p2], keys = ['p1','p2'])
>>> concatenated
```

The components may be retrieved from the combined data by using the keys. As an example:

>>>concatenated.ix['p1']

Data Operations

When you've finished with the missing data, you may do several actions on the data.

Aggregation Operations

You want to do several aggregation operations on a numerical field, such as sum, average, and so on. The following approaches were used to assess it:

Average. To get the average number of obese pupils at the ELEMENTARY school, first, filter the ELEMENTARY data using the command below:

```
>>> data = d[d['GRADE LEVEL'] == 'ELEMENTARY']
213.41593780369291
```

You can now calculate the mean using the following command:

>>>data['NO. OBESE'].mean()

The data object stores and filters basic grade-level data. The NO. OBESE column is selected, which contains the number of obese pupils, and the mean () technique is used to get the average.

SUM.
Use the following command to get the total number of elementary school children who are said to be overweight:

```
>>> data['NO. OBESE'].sum()
219605.0
```

MAX. To find the most significant number of obese students in an elementary school, use the following command:

```
>>> data['NO. OBESE'].max()
48843.0
```

MIN: Use the following command to figure out the fewest number of obese elementary school students:

```
>>> data['NO. OBESE'].min()
5.0
```

STD: Use the following command to get the standard deviation of the number of obese students:

```
>>> data['NO. OBESE'].std()
1690.3831128098113
```

COUNT: Use the following command to determine the total number of elementary schools in DELAWARE county:

```
>>> data = df[(d['GRADE LEVEL'] == 'ELEMENTARY') & (d['COUNTY'] == 'DELAWARE')]
>>> data['COUNTY'].count()
19
```

The tab

The content has been sorted by ELEMENTARY grade and DELAWARE county. See how the criteria are included in parentheses. Because of this, each condition is calculated, and if the parenthesis isn't there, Python will throw an error.

Joins

Pandas can do SQL-like joins on the . Let's create a lookup that will assign levels to each of the grades using the following command:

```
>>> grade_lookup = {'GRADE LEVEL': pd.Series(['ELEMENTARY', 'MIDDLE/HIGH', 'MISC']),'LEVEL': pd.Series([1, 2, 3])}

>>> grade_lookup = DataFrame(grade_lookup)
```

As an example, examine the first five rows of the GRADE data column while computing the joins:

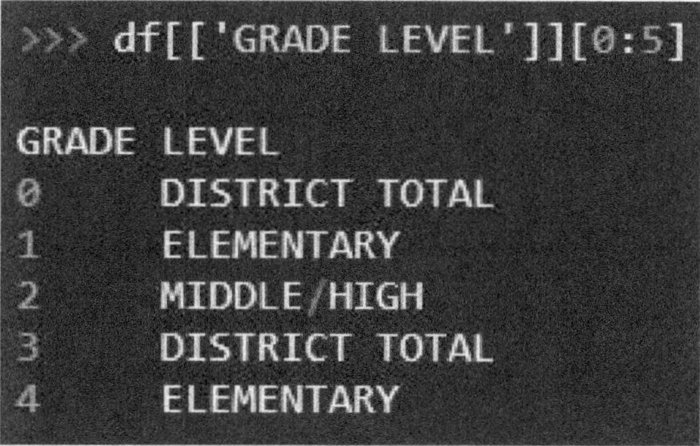

```
>>> df[['GRADE LEVEL']][0:5]

GRADE LEVEL
0        DISTRICT TOTAL
1        ELEMENTARY
2        MIDDLE/HIGH
3        DISTRICT TOTAL
4        ELEMENTARY
```

The Inner Join

The following is an example of an inner join:

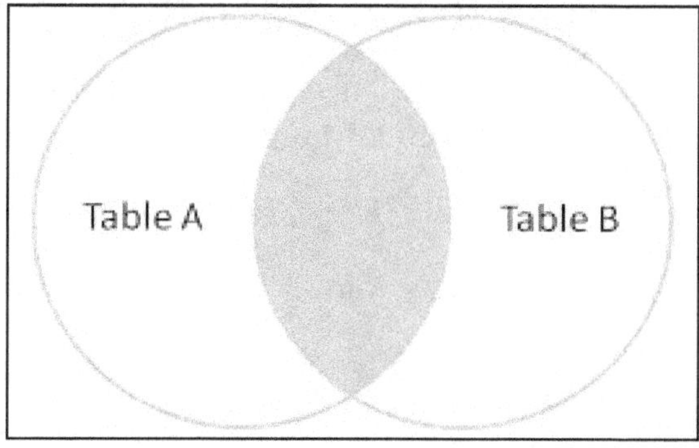

The following command may be used to perform an inner join:

The join () technique is used to perform

```
>>> d_sub = df[0:5].join(grade_lookup.set_index(['GRADE LEVEL']),
on=['GRADE LEVEL'], how='inner')
>>> d_sub[['GRADE LEVEL', 'LEVEL']]
```

the join. The first parameter specifies the DataFrame on which the search will be placed. Note that the index of the grade lookup DataFrame is set using the set index () function. This is required for a join since the join method will not know which column to connect the DataFrame to until this is done.

To connect the data, the second parameter takes a column from the DataFrame. The third option specifies the kind of join as an inner join.

The Left Outer Join

Here's an illustration of the left outer connector.

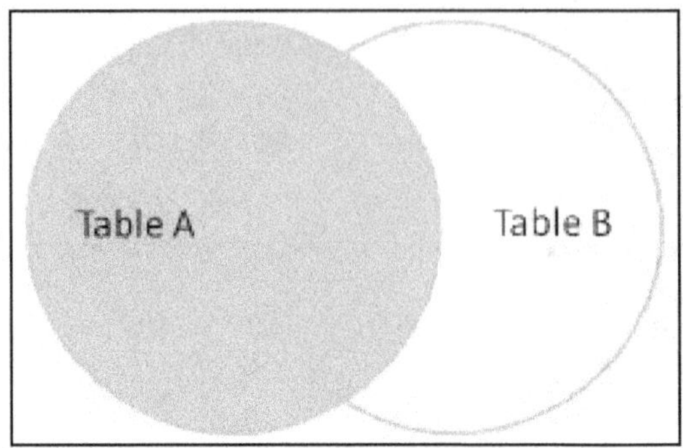

The following instructions may be used to perform an outer join:

```
>>> d_sub = df[0:5].join(grade_lookup.set_index(['GRADE LEVEL']),
on=['GRADE LEVEL'], how='left')
>>> d_sub[['GRADE LEVEL', 'LEVEL']]
```

It is possible to see that the DISTRICT TOTAL has missing data for a level column. There is no instance of DISTRICT TOTAL in the grade lookup Data Frame.

The Full Outer Join

The following is an example of a complete outer join:

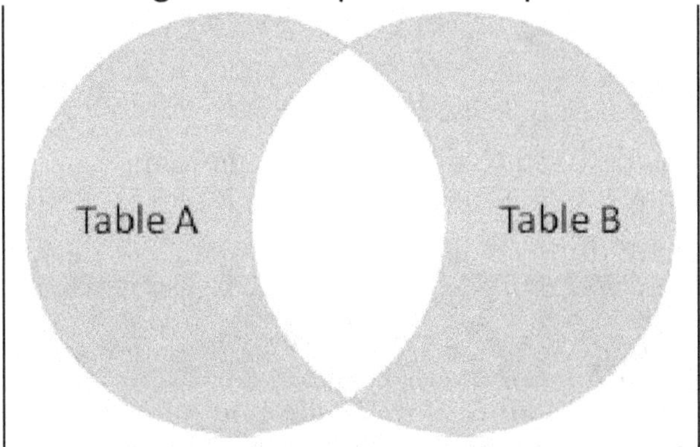

The following instructions may be used to implement the complete outer join:

```
>>> d_sub = df[0:5].join(grade_lookup.set_index(['GRADE LEVEL']),
on=['GRADE LEVEL'], how='outer')
>>> d_sub[['GRADE LEVEL', 'LEVEL']]
```

The Groupby Function

With pandas, it is simple to run a SQL-like group by operation. For example, if you wish to calculate the total number of obese kids in each grade, use the following command:

```
>>> df['NO. OBESE'].groupby(d['GRADE LEVEL']).sum()
 GRADE            LEVEL

DISTRICT TOTAL    127101
ELEMENTARY        72880
MIDDLE/HIGH       53089
```

This command picks the column containing the number of obese students, then applies the group by a technique to group the data-based group level, and finally, the sum method totals the number. The following function can be used to accomplish the same thing:

```
>>> d['NO. OBESE'].groupby(d['GRADE LEVEL']).aggregate(sum)
```

The aggregate approach is used in the preceding example. After the results are obtained, the sum function is called.

It is also feasible to get several forms of aggregations for the same statistic. The following command will achieve this:

```
>>> df['NO. OBESE'].groupby(d['GRADE LEVEL']).aggregate([sum, mean, std])sum mean std
```

To recap, this chapter has covered the fundamentals of the NumPy and pandas libraries. You've learned about the different datatypes in Pandas and how to utilize them. You now understand how to clean and change data. This chapter lays the groundwork for data science, and you may go further into NumPy and pandas.In the next chapter, we'll talk about inferential statistics and how to figure out what different inferential statistics concepts mean.

Chapter 4:

Inferential Statistics

B efore we go into inferential statistics, let's have a look at descriptive statistics. Descriptive statistics is a type of data analysis that sums up the data in a way that is easy to understand so that patterns can be found. It's a simple way to explain facts, but it doesn't help us figure out what to think about the hypothesis. Assume you have a height of 1,000 feet and live in Hong Kong. Their average height would be descriptive data, but it does not disclose that it is the mean height of all of Hong Kong. In this case, you can figure out Hong Kong's average height by using inferential statistics. We'll talk more about this in the next chapter.

In other words, inferential statistics entails explaining the overall picture of the investigation utilizing a restricted quantity of data and drawing inferences from it.

Different Types of Distribution

There are different kinds of probability distributions, and each one shows how likely it is that different things will happen in a random experiment. This section will go through several probability distributions.

The Normal Distribution

This is the most frequent kind of distribution and is commonly used in statistics. Often referred to as a "bell curve" or a "Gaussian curve," after the mathematician Karl Friedrich Gauss. A normal distribution often occurs in nature. Consider the height example we presented at the beginning of the chapter. If you have height data for all persons of a certain gender in Hong Kong and construct a bar chart where each bar reflects the number of people at this exact height, the extracted curve will look like the graph below. The figures in the diagram reflect standard deviations from the mean. It is 0 in the following situation: This notion will become evident as we go through the chapters.

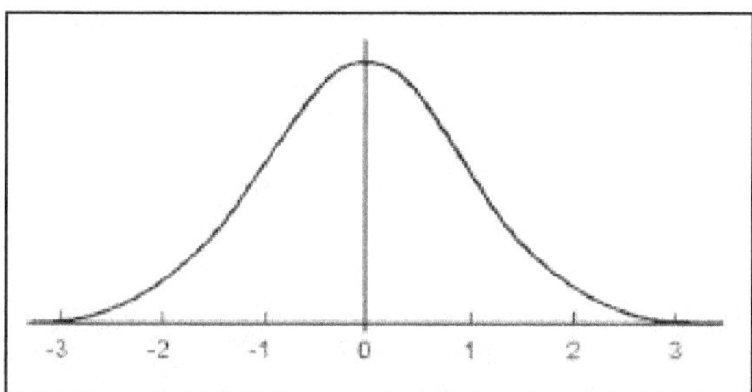

A standard distribution curve can also be seen by looking at an hourglass and how sand builds up when the hourglass is turned upside down. This is a fantastic illustration of how normal distribution appears in nature.

Consider the following diagram: It has three normal distribution curves. The standard deviation of curve A is one, the standard deviation of curve C is two, and the standard deviation of curve B is three. In other words, curve B has the greatest value spread, while curve A has the least value spread. Another point of view is that if curve B reflects the height of people in a country, then this country has a lot of individuals with varied heights, but the country with the curve A distribution will have people whose heights are similar.

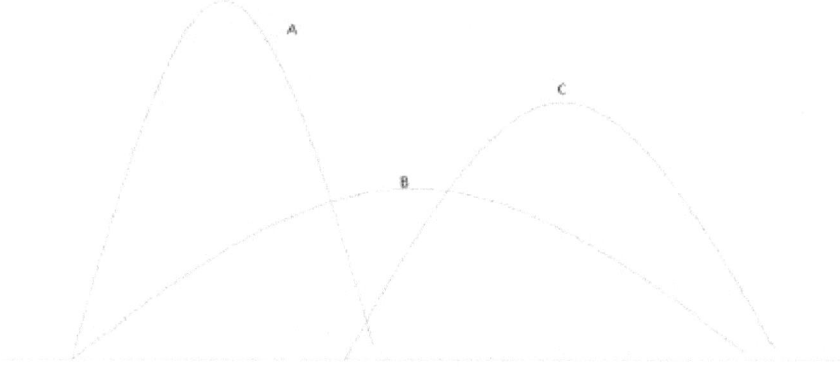

Normal Distribution from a Binomial Distribution
A coin toss has a 50% chance of landing on its head or tail. If you toss the identical coin six times, you can calculate the chance of seeing ahead three times using the method below:

$$P(x) = \frac{n!}{x!(n-x)!} p^x q^{n-x}$$

The predicted number of successes is X.
In the formula above, n represents the number of times the coin is thrown, p is the possibility of success, and q is (1-p), which represents the likelihood of failure.

The SciPy module in Python contains useful utilities for completing statistical calculations. It is available at http://www.scipy.org/.
You may plot the binomial distribution with these instructions.

```python
>>> from scipy.stats import binom
>>> import matplotlib.pyplot as plt
>>> fig, ax = plt.subplots(1, 1)
>>> x = [0, 1, 2, 3, 4, 5, 6]
>>> n, p = 6, 0.5
>>> rv = binom(n, p)
>>> ax.vlines(x, 0, rv.pmf(x), colors='k', linestyles='-', lw=1,
label='Probablity')
>>> ax.legend(loc='best', frameon=False)
>>> plt.show()
```

The binom function creates binomial distributions and the statistics associated with them. If you look at the preceding instructions, you'll see that several of them are derived from matplotlib, which you'll use now to plot the binomial distribution. In the next chapters, you will learn more about the matplotlib library. The plt.subplots method is helpful in creating graphs on a screen. The binom function takes into account the number of tries as well as the possibility of success. The ax.vlines function is used to make vertical lines, and the rv.pmf function is used to figure out the probability for different x values. The ax.legend method adds a legend to the graph, and plt.show displays it. The end result is as follows:

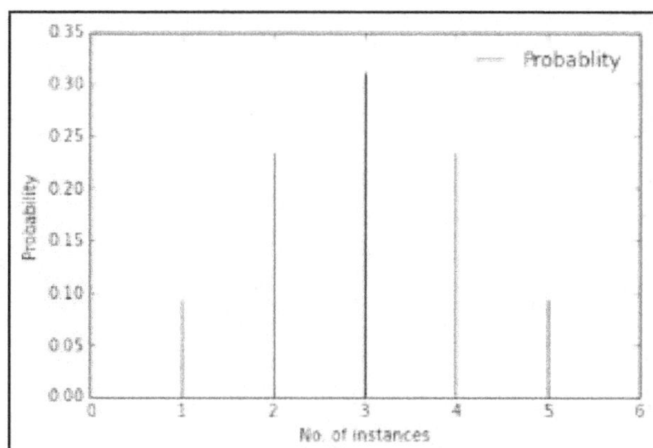

According to the graph above, if the coin is thrown six times, the likelihood of finding three heads is the greatest, while gaining single or five heads have the lowest probability.

What if we raise the number of tries to 100? What will the distribution look like?

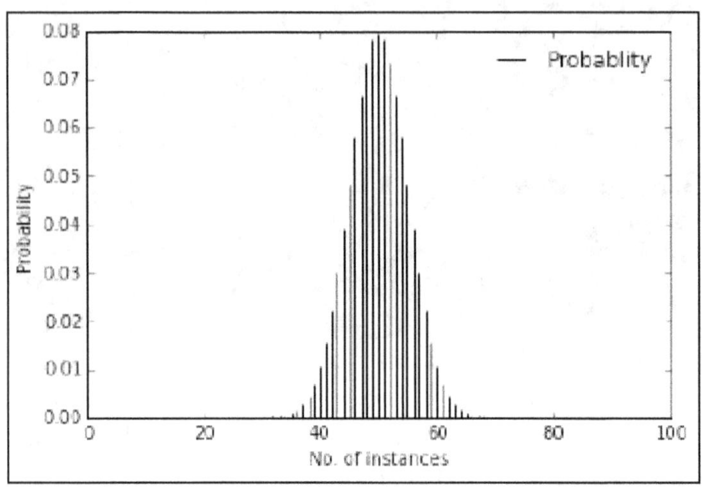

When the probability of success is set to 0.4, you will see the following:

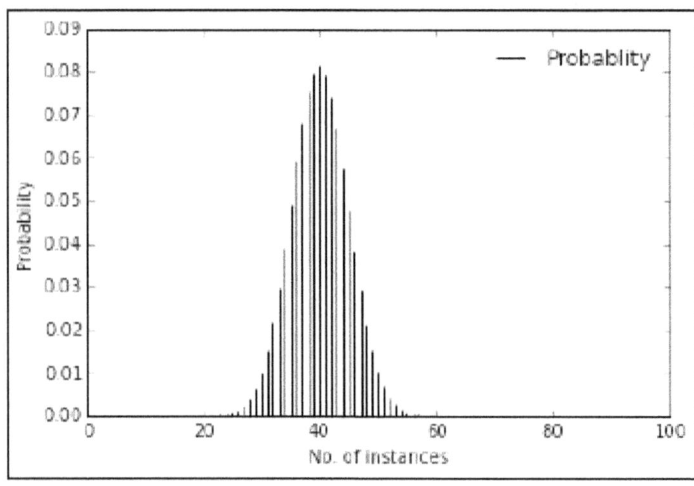

And when you toss the coin 1000 times with a chance of 0.5.
You will get the following:

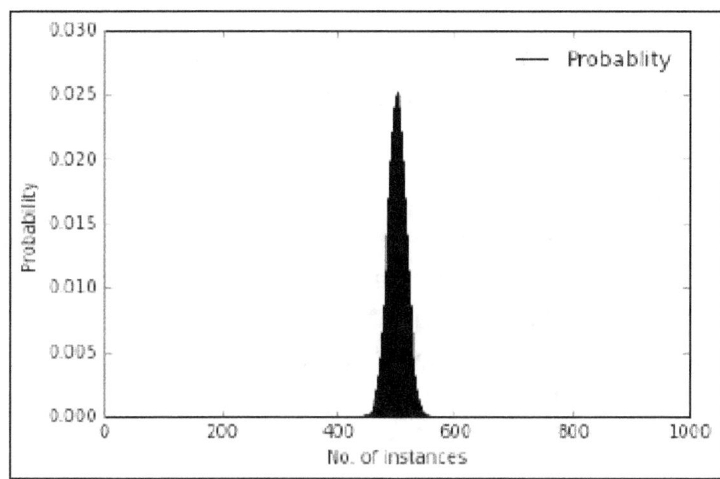

Do you see how the binomial distribution is beginning to resemble a normal distribution?

The Poisson Distribution

The probability distribution of self-determining interval occurrences in an interval is referred to here. The binomial distribution is used to calculate the likelihood of binary occurrences, while the Poisson distribution is helpful for count-based distributions. If lambda is the average occurrence of events per interval, then this formula provides the likelihood of receiving a k occurrence during a given period:

$$f(k;\lambda) = \Pr(X = k) = \frac{\lambda^k e^{-\lambda}}{k!}$$

In the following formula, e represents Euler's number, k represents the total number of occurrences for which the probability will be calculated, and lambda represents the mean number of occurrences.

Let me provide an example to demonstrate this; there are 20 autos that pass via a bridge in one hour. What are the chances of 23 automobiles passing under the bridge in an hour?

For this example, we'll use SciPy's Poisson function:

```
>>> from scipy.stats import poisson
>>> rv = poisson(20)
>>> rv.pmf(23)
```

The Poisson function is used to calculate the mean value, which is 20 automobiles. The likelihood is shown by the rv.pmf function, which is around 6%.

The Bernoulli distribution

An experiment may have two potential outcomes: success or failure. The chance of success is indicated by p, while the probability of failure is denoted by 1-p. The Bernoulli distribution is described as a random variable with the value 1 indicating success and 0 indicating failure. This is the probability distribution formula:

$$P(n) = p^n (1-p)^{1-n}$$

Also known as:

$$P(n) = \begin{cases} 1-p & \text{for } n = 0 \\ p & \text{for } n = 1 \end{cases}$$

The following graph depicts the Bernoulli distribution:

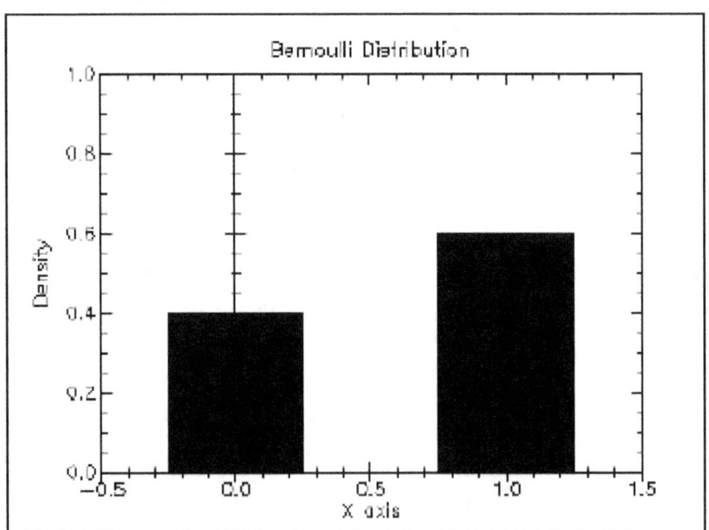

Voting in an election is a wonderful illustration of the Bernoulli distribution. The SciPY package's bernoulli.rvs () function may be used to generate the Bernoulli distribution. With a probability of 0.7, this function creates a Bernoulli distribution.

```
>>> from scipy import stats
>>> stats.bernoulli.rvs(0.7, size=100)
array([1, 1, 1, 1, 1, 0, 0, 1, 1, 0, 1, 1, 1, 0, 1, 1, 1, 1, 1, 1, 1,
1, 0,
1, 1, 1, 0, 1, 1, 0, 1, 0, 0, 1, 0, 0, 1, 0, 1, 0, 1, 1, 1, 1,
1, 0,
1, 1, 1, 1, 1, 0, 0, 1, 1, 1, 0, 1, 0, 1, 0, 0, 0, 0, 0, 1, 0,
0, 0,
1, 1, 1, 0, 1, 0, 1, 1, 1, 1, 1, 1, 0, 0, 1, 1, 1, 0, 0, 0, 1,
1, 1,
1, 0, 1, 1, 1, 0, 1, 1])
```

If the above output reflects the number of votes cast for a candidate,
the candidate receives 70% of the vote.

The A-Z Score

Simply said, this is a score that indicates the value of the distribution in
standard deviations from the average. Consider the following formula
for calculating the z-score:

$$z = (X - \mu) / \sigma$$

In the following example, X represents the distribution value, u
represents the distribution mean, and symbolizes the distribution
standard deviation.

Let's use a school classroom as an example to convey this topic.

Imagine you have a class of 60 pupils who have just gotten their maths
test results. Now, using the following command, we mimic the scores of
these 60 students using a normal distribution:

```
>>> classscore
>>> classscore = np.random.normal(50, 10, 60).round()
[ 56. 52. 60. 65. 39. 49. 41. 51. 48. 52. 47. 41. 60.
54. 41.
46. 37. 50. 50. 55. 47. 53. 38. 42. 42. 57. 40. 45.
35. 39.
67. 56. 35. 45. 47. 52. 48. 53. 53. 50. 61. 60. 57.
53. 56.
68. 43. 35. 45. 42. 33. 43. 49. 54. 45. 54. 48. 55.
56. 30.]
```

The NumPy package includes a random module with a regular function,
where 50 is the mean of the distribution, 10 is the standard deviation,

and 60 is the number of values to be created. The normal distribution
may be plotted using the following commands:

```
>>> plt.hist(classscore, 30, normed=True) #Number of breaks is 30
>>> plt.show()
```

The following functions may be used to convert each student's score to
a z-score:

```
>>> stats.zscore(classscore)

[ 0.86008868  0.38555699  1.33462036  1.92778497 -1.15667098
  0.02965823
 -0.91940514  0.26692407 -0.08897469  0.38555699 -0.20760761 -
  0.91940514
  1.33462036  0.62282284 -0.91940514 -0.32624053 -1.39393683
  0.14829115
  0.14829115  0.74145576 -0.20760761  0.50418992 -1.2753039  -
  0.80077222
 -0.80077222  0.9787216  -1.03803806 -0.44487345 -1.63120267 -
  1.15667098
  2.16505081  0.86008868 -1.63120267 -0.44487345 -0.20760761
  0.38555699
 -0.08897469  0.50418992  0.50418992  0.14829115  1.45325329
  1.33462036
  0.9787216   0.50418992  0.86008868  2.28368373 -0.6821393   -
  1.63120267
 -0.44487345 -0.80077222 -1.86846851 -0.6821393   0.02965823
  0.62282284
 -0.44487345  0.62282284 -0.08897469  0.74145576  0.86008868  -
  2.22436727]
```

In the following example, a student with a zscore of 1.334 has a score of
60 out of 100. The conventional normal table will be used to make sense
of the z-score.

This table helps in determining the likelihood of a score.
It is critical to understand that the likelihood of obtaining a score higher
than 60 is:

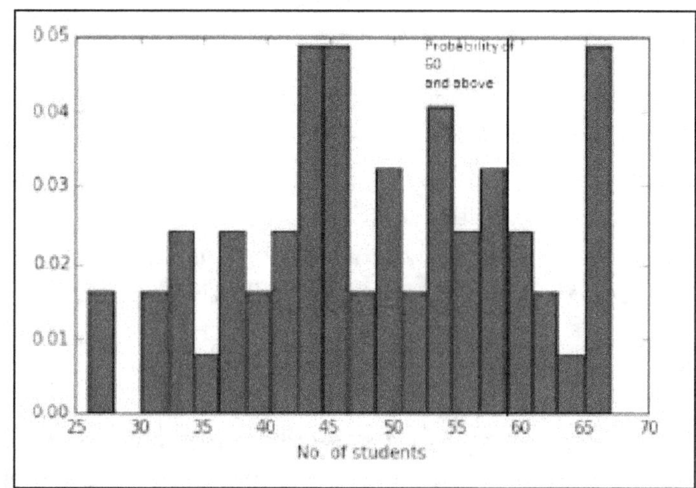

The regular table might help you figure out how likely it is that the score will happen, but you don't have to go through the table and figure out the probability to find the value. The cdf function, or cumulative distribution function, makes this work easier:

```
>>> prob = 1 - stats.norm.cdf(1.334)
>>> prob
0.091101928265359899
```

The cdf function indicates the likelihood of obtaining values up to the z-score of 1.334, and subtracting one from it gives the chance of gaining a z-score more significant than it. This suggests that the likelihood of receiving marks over 60 is 0.09.

Here's another question: "How many students made it to the top 20% of the class?"

For this question, you must work backwards to discover the marks at which all of the students above it are in the top 20% of the class.

To acquire the z-score at which the top 20% score marks, use SciPy'sppf function:

```
>>> stats.norm.ppf(0.80)
0.84162123357291435
```

The z-score for the preceding output, which determines whether the top 20% of marks are received, is 0.84, as shown below:

```
>>> (0.84 * classscore.std()) + classscore.mean()
```

55.9425941765242267

You multiply the z-score by the standard deviation and then add the result to the distribution's average. This helps in converting the z-score to a distribution value. The 55.83 points indicate that students who scored higher are in the top 20% of the distribution.

The z-score is a widely used and significant concept in statistics. Now you can see how it is used to standardize any distribution so that it can be compared to it.

A P-value

A p-value is a chance that a null hypothesis will be thrown out when it turns out to be true. The null hypothesis asserts that there is no difference between the two metrics. If the hypothesis is correct, persons who study for 4 hours each day will get more than 90 points out of 100. In this situation, the null hypothesis would be that there is no relationship between the number of hours worked and the marks earned.

If the p-value is equal to or less than the significance threshold (a), the null hypothesis is wrong and must be rejected.

Let's take a look at an example where the null hypothesis is that students usually get 68 in math.

Let's get the z-score of 68 points:

```
>>> zscore = ( 68 - classscore.mean() ) / classscore.std()
>>> zscore
2.283
```

Let us now calculate the value:

```
>>> prob = 1 - stats.norm.cdf(zscore)
>>> prob
0.032835182628040638
```

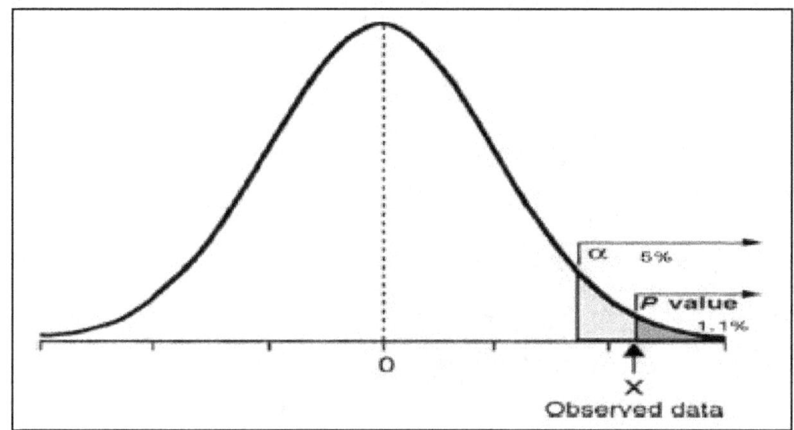

As a result, the p-value is 3.2%, which is lower than the significance threshold. In other words, the null hypothesis may not be true, and it can be inferred that getting 68 points in math is unusual.

One-Tailed and Two-Tailed Tests

In a two-tailed test, the hypothesis is determined by using both tails of the null hypothesis.

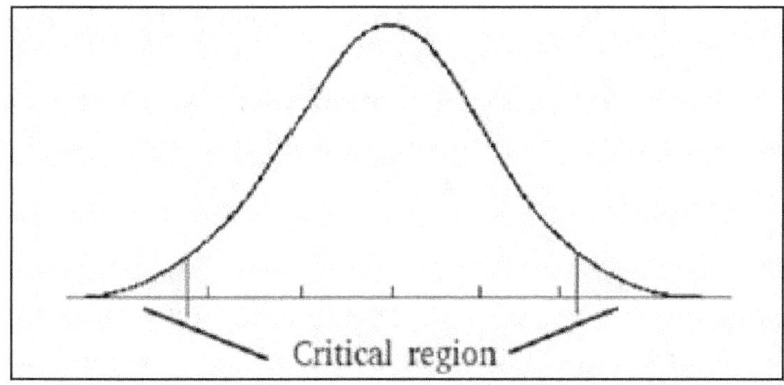

When a percentage of 5% is used in a two-tailed test, it is distributed equally on both sides. In this situation, it's 2.5% on one side and 2.5% on the other.

Here's an example to help you understand. The average score on the national math test is 60, and the standard deviation is 3 points.

A class's average grade is 53. The null hypothesis is about the average grade in the class, which is the same as the average grade in the country.

To begin, let us test the following hypothesis by first determining the z-score of 60.

```
>>> zscore = ( 53 - 60 ) / 3.0
>>> zscore
-2.3333333333333335
```

The p-value would be as follows:

```
>>> prob = stats.norm.cdf(zscore)
>>> prob
0.009815328862864533336
```

The p-value in this situation is 0.98%. The null hypothesis must be rejected, and the p-value in either direction of the bell curve must be less than 2.5%. Since the p-value is less than 2.5%, you may reject the null hypothesis and describe how the class's average marks vary from the national average.

Type 1 and Type 2 Errors

"Type 1 error" is the mistake that happens when the null hypothesis is thrown out even though it is clear that it is true. This is referred to as a first-kind mistake and is equal to false positives.

Let us provide an example to explain this notion. Imagine that a new medicine is being made and that it needs to be tested to see how well it works against diseases. The null hypothesis states that it is ineffective in combating illnesses.

The significance threshold is kept at 5% such that the null hypothesis may be accepted with confidence 95% of the time. Yet, 5% of the time, you will accept the hypothesis's rejection even though it must be accepted. In other words, its effectiveness is presumed even if the medicine is unsuccessful.

Controlling the relevance level, alpha, regulates the Type 1 mistake. Alpha has the greatest likelihood of a Type 1 mistake.

The smaller the alpha value, the lesser the Type 1 mistake.

When you do not reject a false null hypothesis, you commit a Type 2 mistake.

In the field of pharmacology, this kind of mistake happens when the medicine is said to be useless when it actually works.
This kind of issue may be controlled one at a time. As one of the mistakes is reduced, the other grows. The analysis tries to focus on the application and the issue statement, and as a result, the correct mistake should be less likely to happen. A Type 1 mistake should be minimized in this medication situation since sending a reliably effective medicine is preferable.

A Confidence Interval
In statistics, the confidence interval refers to the population component. The confidence interval helps in determining the level for calculating the population mean.
Assuming 50 males have the following heights in centimeters:

```
>>> height_data = np.array([ 186.0, 180.0, 195.0, 189.0, 191.0,
177.0, 161.0, 177.0, 192.0, 182.0, 185.0, 192.0,
173.0, 172.0, 191.0, 184.0, 193.0, 182.0, 190.0, 185.0, 181.0,
188.0, 179.0, 188.0,
170.0, 179.0, 180.0, 189.0, 188.0, 185.0, 170.0, 197.0, 187.0,
182.0, 173.0, 179.0,
184.0, 177.0, 190.0, 174.0, 203.0, 206.0, 173.0, 169.0, 178.0,
201.0, 198.0, 166.0,
171.0, 180.0])
```

When the distribution is plotted, it has a normal distribution:

```
>>> plt.hist(height_data, 30, normed=True)
>>> plt.show()
```

The distribution's average includes:
>>>height_data.mean()
183.24000000000001

As a result, the average height of a male in the sample is 183.4 cm.
To figure out the confidence interval, you will now give the standard error of the mean.

The standard error of the mean is the distance between the sample mean, and the population means. It is defined using the following formula:

$$SE_{\bar{x}} = \frac{s}{\sqrt{n}}$$

In the example below, s is the standard deviation of the sample, and n is the number of items in the sample.
This may be calculated using the SciPy package's sem() function:
>>>stats.sem(height_data)
1.37871871900005252

As a result, the standard error of the mean is 1.38cm. Entering this calculation yields the bottom and upper bounds of the confidence interval.

```
Upper/Lower limit = mean(height) + / - sigma * SEmean(x)
```

Thus, for the lower limit:
183.24 + (1.96 * 1.38) = 185.94
And for upper limit:
183.24 - (1.96*1.38) = 180.53
At 1.96 standard deviation occupies 95% of the area in the normal distribution.

We can confidently consider the population mean to be between 180.53 and 185.94cm of the height.

Imagine we now pick a sample of 50 persons, record their heights, and repeat the procedure 30 times. The distribution may then be seen by plotting the averages of each sample.

The following instructions were used to replicate the above plot:

```python
>>> average_height = []
>>> for i in xrange(30):
>>> sample50 = np.random.normal(183, 10, 50).round()
>>> average_height.append(sample50.mean())
>>> plt.hist(average_height, 20, normed=True)
>>> plt.show()
```

When you replicate the mean height of 50 males who were measured 30 times, you should see that the mean varies from 180 to 187 cm.
If you get 100 males and repeat the method 30 times:

```python
>>> average_height = []
>>> for i in xrange(30):
>>> sample1000 = np.random.normal(183, 10, 1000).round()
>>> average_height.append(sample1000.mean())
>>> plt.hist(average_height, 10, normed=True)
>>> plt.show()
```

As you may have seen, the height changes from 182.4cm to 183.4cm. What does this symbolize?

In other words, as the sample size rises, the standard error of the mean reduces, resulting in a narrowing of the confidence range and the ability to predict the interval in which the population means would fall.

Correlation

Correlation in statistics refers to the resemblance between two random variables. The most common type of correlation is between two people, which is shown by the following formula:

$$\rho_{X,Y} = \frac{\text{cov}(X,Y)}{\sigma_X \sigma_Y} = \frac{E\left[(X - \mu_X)(Y - \mu_Y)\right]}{\sigma_X \sigma_Y}$$

```
>>> mpg = [21.0, 21.0, 22.8, 21.4, 18.7, 18.1, 14.3, 24.4, 22.8,
19.2, 17.8, 16.4, 17.3, 15.2, 10.4, 10.4, 14.7, 32.4, 30.4,
33.9, 21.5, 15.5, 15.2, 13.3, 19.2, 27.3, 26.0, 30.4, 15.8,
19.7, 15.0, 21.4]
>>> hp = [110, 110, 93, 110, 175, 105, 245, 62, 95, 123, 123, 180,
180, 180, 205, 215, 230, 66, 52, 65, 97, 150, 150, 245,
175, 66, 91, 113, 264, 175, 335, 109]
>>> stats.pearsonr(mpg,hp)
(-0.77616837182658638, 1.7878352541210661e-07)
```

The relationship between horsepower and mileage is shown by the first value of the output. The pvalue is shown by the second value.

As a result, the first value suggests that it is substantially adversely related, while the p-value indicates that there is a significant association between them.

The plot diagram is as follows:

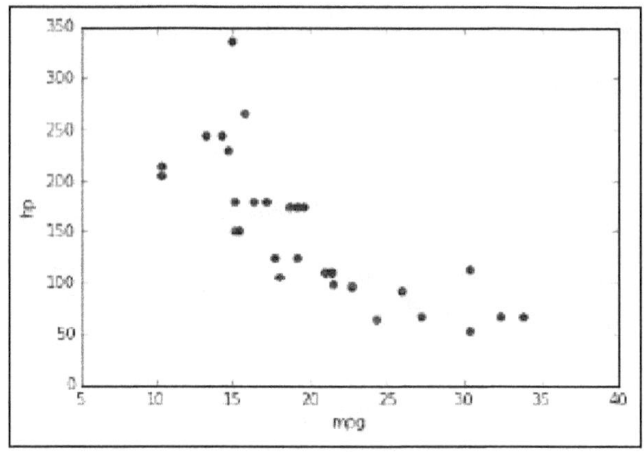

The graphic above shows that the mpg improves when the horsepower decreases.

Consider another kind of correlation, the Spearman correlation. The following correlation holds for the rank order of the values, making the relationship between the two distributions constant. It is useful for ordinal data and is unaffected by outliers.

Let's look at the Spearman association between MPG and horsepower. This is possible using the SciPy package's spearmanr() function:

```
>>> stats.spearmanr(mpg,hp)
(-0.89466464574996252, 5.085969430924539e-12)
```

It's worth noting that the Spearman correlation is -0.89, and the pvalue is significant.

Let's do an experiment in which we add different outlier values to the data and see how the Pearson and Spearman correlations change.

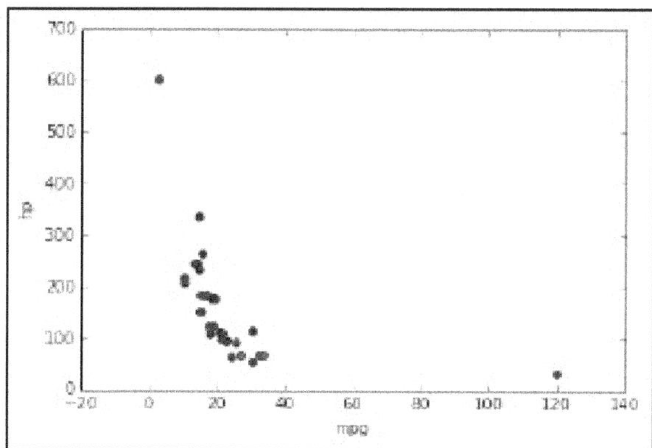

The prior figure clearly defines the outlier values.
Consider how Pearson and Spearman's correlations influence the correlations.

The Pearson correlation is represented by the following commands:

```
>>> stats.pearsonr(mpg, hp)
>>> (-0.47415304891435484, 0.0046122167947348462)
```

The Spearman correlation is as follows:

```
>>> stats.spearmanr(mpg,hp)
(-0.89466464574996252, 5.085969430924539e-12)
```

The outliers, which range from a correlation of 0.89 to 0.47, have had an effect on the Pearson correlation.

Even though the Spearman correlation is based on the order of the data instead of the actual value, it doesn't change.
Z-test vs T-test

Before validating your null hypothesis, you performed many Z-tests.

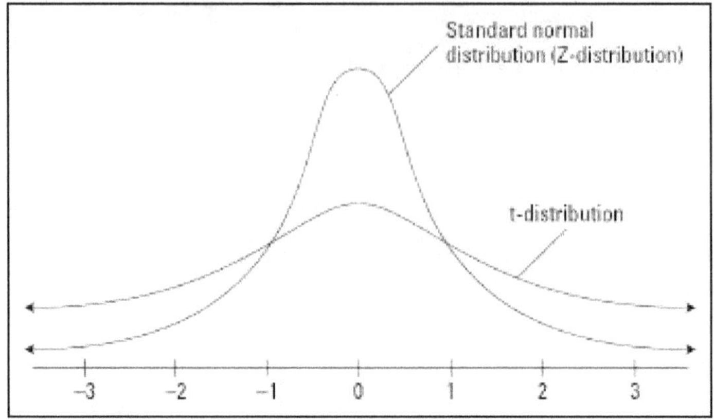

A T-distribution is similar to a Z-distribution. The standard deviation of T-distributions is always proportionately bigger than that of Z-distributions.
When the number of people in the sample is small, the t distribution is often used to figure out what the population is like.

The Z-test compares the population means to a sample to the population mean of two distributions with a sample size higher than 30. The Z-test, for example, would compare the heights of males from different ethnic groups.

The T-test is used to compare the population average to a sample or to compare the population mean of two distributions when the sample size is less than 30 and when the population's standard deviation is unknown.

The F Distribution
This distribution is also known as Snedecor's F distribution.
The following formula yields an F static.

$$f = \left[s_1^2 / \sigma_1^2 \right] / \left[s_2^2 / \sigma_2^2 \right]$$

In the following example, s1 denotes the standard deviation of sample 1 with n1, size, s2, and sample 2's standard deviation. The F distribution is the distribution of all possible values of f statistics. In this graphic, d1 and d2 denote the degrees of freedom:

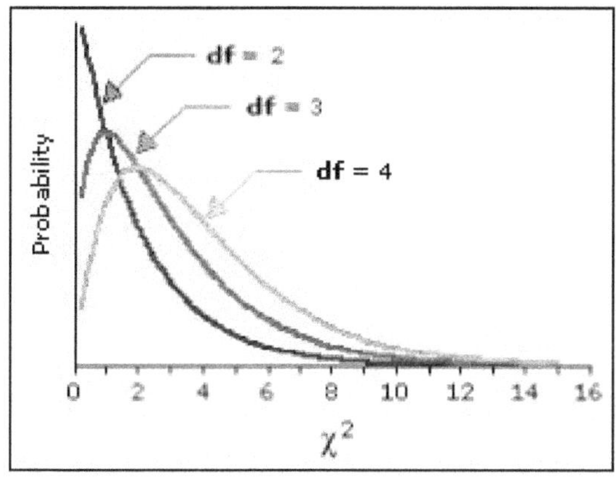

The Chi-Square Distribution
The following formula defines this sort of distribution:

$$X^2 = \left[(n-1)*s^2\right]/\sigma^2$$

In the following example, n is the size of the sample, s is the standard deviation of the sample, and is the standard deviation of the whole population.

If you take samples and define the chi-square statistics regularly, you may get a chi-square distribution, which is defined by the probability function:

$$Y = Y_0 * \left(X^2\right)^{(v/2-1)} * e^{-X2/2}$$

Chi-Square for the Goodness of Fit
The Chi-square test can be used to find out if the data that was collected is very different from the data that was planned. For example, if the dice are rolled 36 times, the probability that each face would show up is 1/6. As a result, the following is the predicted distribution:

Expected Frequency	Outcome
6	1
6	2
6	3

6	4
6	5
6	6

The observed distribution consists of the following:

Observed Frequency	Outcome
7	1
5	2
3	3
9	4
6	5
6	6

The null hypothesis for the chi-square test is that the observed value is about the same as the expected value.

The chi-square test may be performed using the SciPy package's chi-

square function:

```
>>> stats.chisquare(observed,expected)
(3.333333333333333, 0.64874235866759344
```

The first number is the chi-square value, while the second is the exceedingly high pvalue. In other words, the null hypothesis is true, and the value that was seen matches the value that was predicted.

Chapter 5:

Python Libraries-Pygal

Why Should You Use Pygal?

There are several libraries for charts in Python programming (Matplotlib and plotly are two examples), and many resources have been made for many of them. Since this is an introduction to data charts, you need a library that is easy to use so that even a beginner can follow the code.

The Kozea community created Pygal, a Python-based SVG Charts maker. This community is dedicated to creating high-quality open-source libraries, mostly in Python.

In addition to traditional charts, the Pygal library has line charts, pie graphs, and bar graphs that can be used to make charts.
It includes a global map as well as radar charts, box plots, and funnel charts.

It also comes with prebuilt themes and styles that you don't have to change if you don't have to. Also, since the output of the chart library is SVG, it can be used for both HTML5 and print. One issue with some Python chart libraries is that the output defaults to the PNG format with a specific picture size. Since SVG is a vector graphic, it can be shrunk or enlarged to fit any need without losing quality.
You may visit the website at http://pygal.org/.

The documentation on the Pygal website is lovely and simple to read. The documentation for third-party Python libraries may range from a well-documented, online-searchable wiki to a basic readme.txt file that just explains how to install the library. Also, the Pygal library does not need many dependencies, which is crucial for an introductory book.
Several Python frameworks have fussy dependencies that you may need for your project, but they might or might not function with your system.
The only library necessary for pygal is the lxml library, although it has many difficulties depending on the operating system on which you are running your Python code. It is critical that you read the lxml notes again before proceeding with the pygal installation.
Pygal Installation Using Pip

First, if you haven't already done so, install the lxml installer if you're using Windows. Alternatively, the steps below should assist you in installing lxml. After that, you can install pip and pygal on both Mac and Windows by following the steps below.
Enter the following instructions if you are using a Windows laptop:

install pygal using pip
If you're using Ubuntu, use the following command:
pygalsudo pip install

Next, launch Eclipse with PyDev and create a new Python project. When you've created the project, make a new file called importtest.py and run the following command:
Bring in pygal.

After you're finished, use CTRL + Space to view PyDev's code. In this screenshot, pygal is being reconfigured in the system:

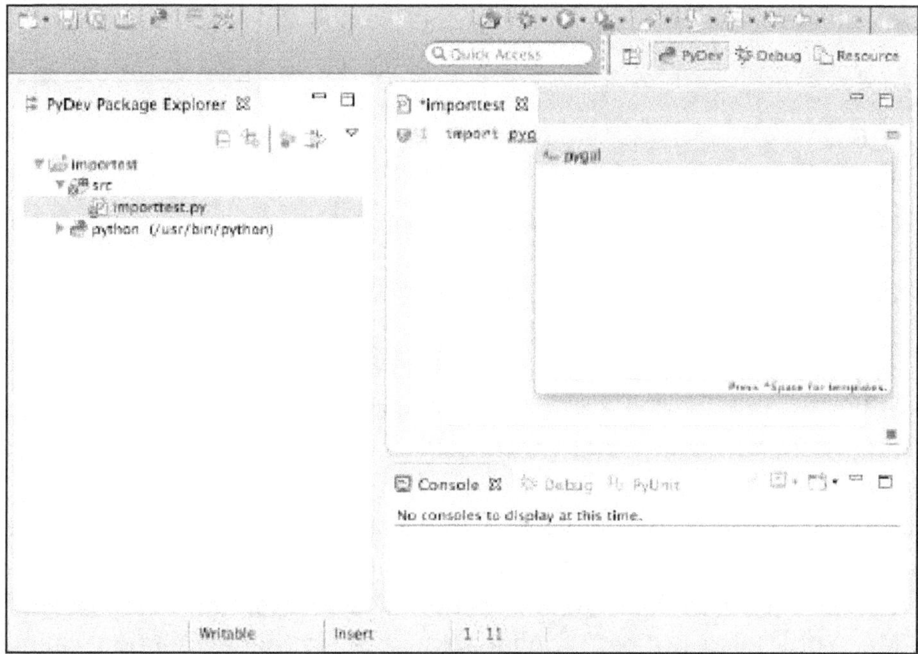

Install Pygal Using Python Tools for Visual Studio

If you intend to utilize Visual Studio, here's some installation advice. First, if you haven't already, execute an easy install using your Python environment in the install Python Package window, as seen in the picture below:

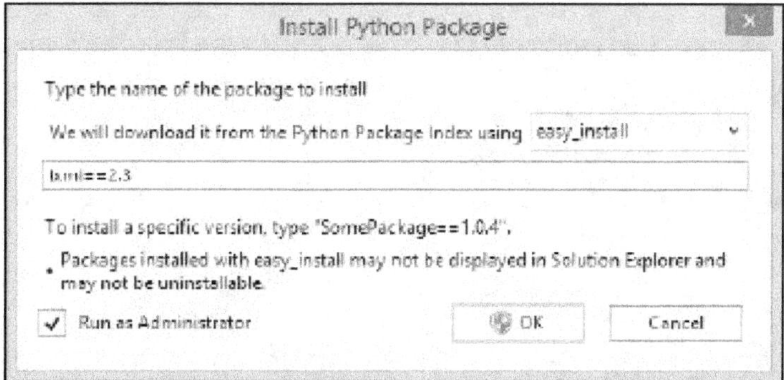

If everything goes OK, install the pygal library. Right-click inside your environments and choose to install the python package, this time choosing pygal, as seen in the screenshot:

Install Python Package

Type the name of the package to install

We will download it from the Python Package Index using pip

pygal

To install a specific version, type 'SomePackage==1.0.4'.

☑ Run as Administrator   OK   Cancel

Creating a Line Chart

Line charts generally show how a particular piece of data evolves over time. This is the most basic chart you can make when it comes to charting. It has x and y axes; each axis on the chart represents time, value, or a separate parameter.

Let's make a basic graph showing the number of visitors to a website over the last two years. Examine the first line of this code. The Python interpreter uses a declarative line to define the string encoding type of the file. You'll also notice it online. You use an inline function called range on x labels ().

This lets you make an array of integers that go from smallest to biggest. In this scenario, 2012 and 2014 would result in an array of 2012, 2013, and 2014. Now, paste the following code into the main Python file of your project:

```python
# -*- coding: utf-8 -*-
import pygal
#create a new line chart.
line = pygal.Line()
line.title = 'Website hits in the past 2 years' #set chart title
line.x_labels = map(str, range(2012, 2014)) #set the x-axis labels.
line.add('Page views', [None, 0, 12, 32, 72, 148]) #set values.
line.render_to_file('linechart.svg') #set filename.
```

A simple pygal line chart output is shown in the picture below:

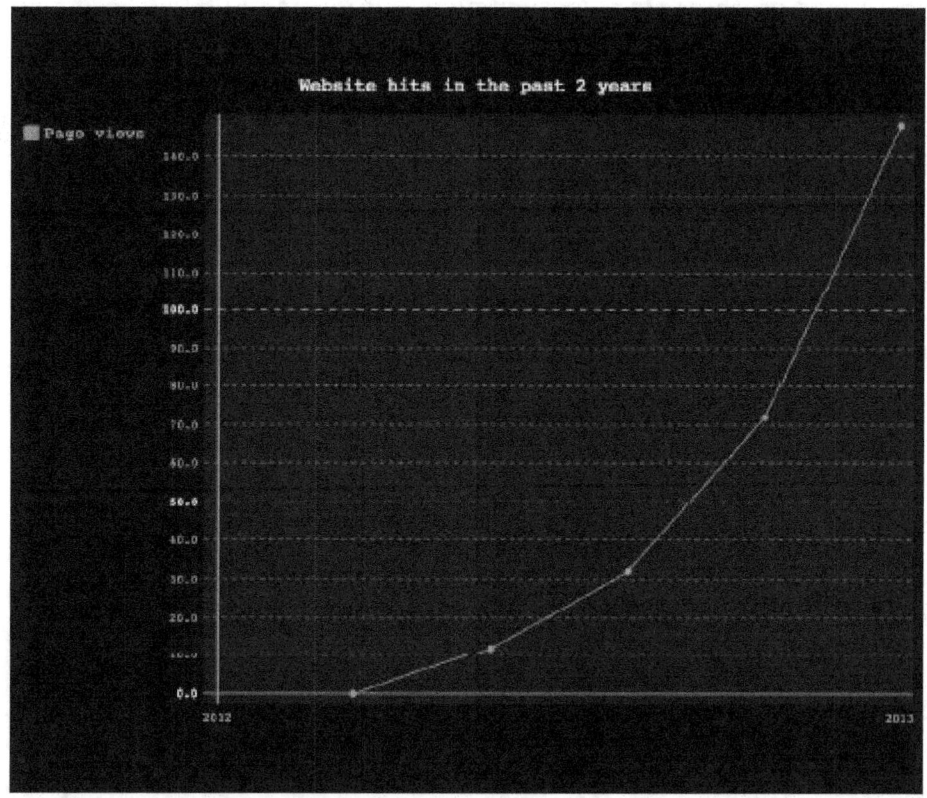

The linechart.SVG file should be produced within the main project file where you run your script. After you open this file, your character will appear like the one in the screenshot above. To find the file, go to your project's directory and look for the linechart.svg file. Remember that you may hover over the dots to get the values of each marker in the chart. These are some of the attributes included with the pygal library.

You'll also see that the chars' chronology starts at 0.0 in 2013. The first argument in the line.add() expression is None. This inserts a spacer inside the chart, pushing the data out rather than forcing the chart to start in 2012. This is a common method for creating chart layouts.

Another feature is that when you hover your mouse over the line label, the entry line is highlighted, describing the dataset you're seeing with that label. The pygal package will also examine your data and stress-specific lines on the data axis, such as o.0, 50.0, and 100.0, in order to break up numerous chart lines for easy comprehension.

The kind of IDE you use determines the code hinting capability for pygal's line () function. The pygal library is written differently than other Python libraries. Using a for loop, the software dynamically creates each chart style. This loop validates every chart class in the pygal library. So, IDEs that need static, hardcoded Python methods will throw an error when they are called, but they won't crash. This implies that code hinting may or may not function correctly, depending on the editor you're using.

Stacked Line Charts

Stacked line charts function similarly to standard line charts. The main exception is that it stacks many pieces of data on top of each other. In your Python file, paste the following code and run it.

```python
# -*- coding: utf-8 -*-
import pygal
#create a new stacked line chart.
line = pygal.StackedLine(fill=True)
line.title = 'Web hits in the past 2 years' #set chart title
line.x_labels = map(str, range(2012, 2014)) #set the x-axis labels.
line.add('Site A', [None, 0, 12, 32, 72, 148]) #set values.
line.add('Site B', [2, 16, 12, 87, 91, 342]) #set values.
line.add('Site C', [42, 55, 84, 88, 90, 171]) #set values.
line.render_to_file('linechart.svg') #set filename.
```

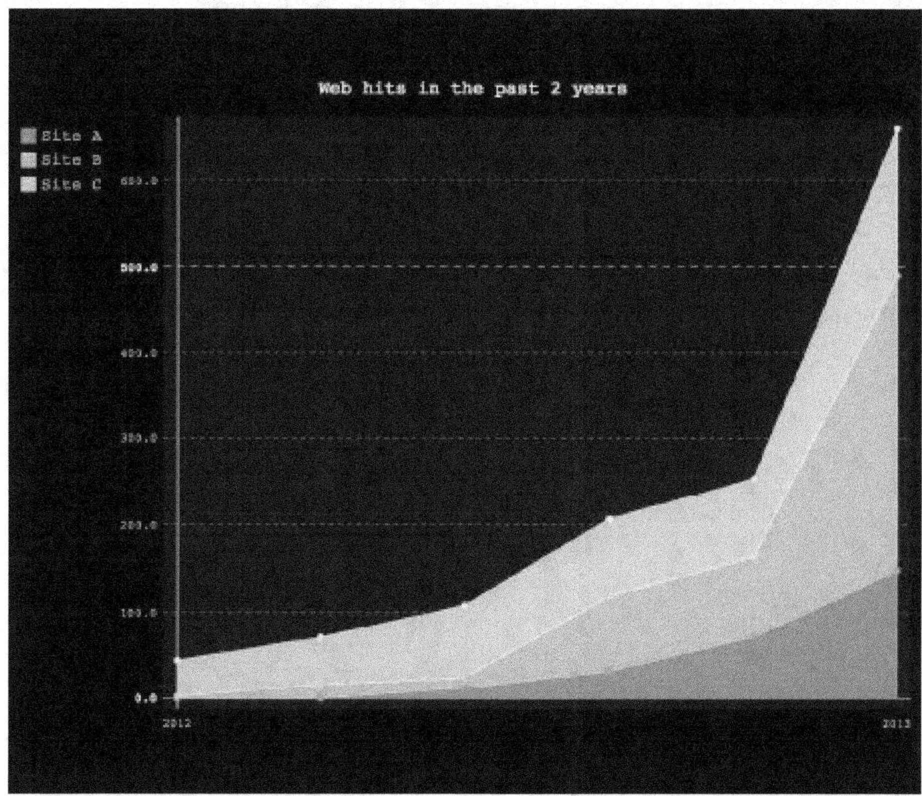

After deployed, your stacked chart should look like the one in the prior picture. To find the linechart.svg file, go to the directory where your project is located. Remember how pygal overrides your first SVG file by default when dealing with the following libraries. When you define your chart, you will see that you included a fill = True argument to the Stacked Line function; this is a chart parameter.

Simple Bar Charts

The use of basic bar charts is similar to that of line charts.

It also assigns values to information categories. To make a basic bar chart, use the code below.

```python
# -*- coding: utf-8 -*-
import pygal
#create a new bar chart.
bar = pygal.Bar()
bar.title = 'Searches for term: sleep'
bar.x_labels = map(str, range(2011, 2015))
bar.add('Searches', [81, 88, 88, 100])
bar.render_to_file('bar_chart.svg')
```

Go to your project directory and open your browser to see the bar chart.svg. Remember that the code hasn't changed much. The results are shown in the image below:

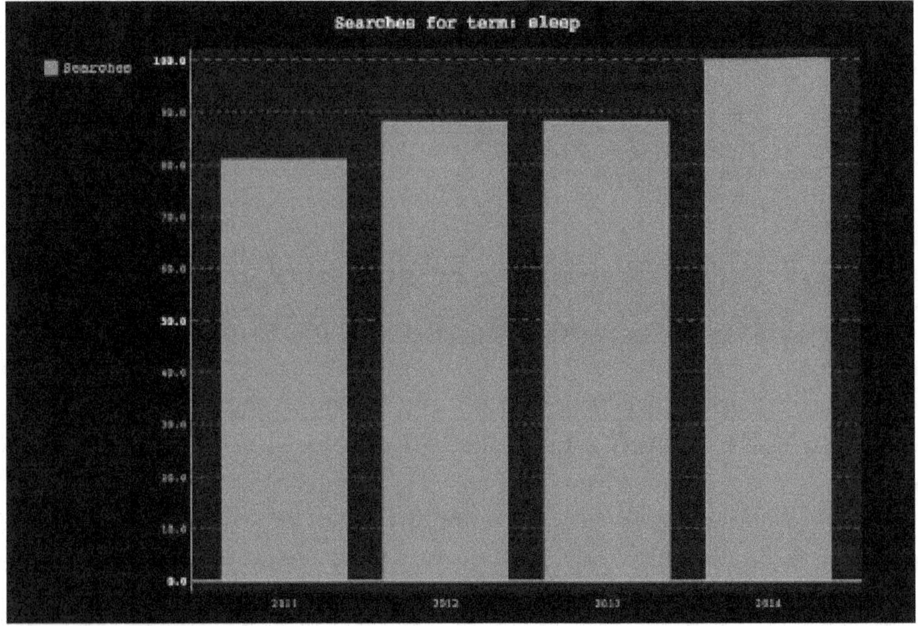

Stacked Bar Charts

Stacked bar charts, like line charts, layer various bars one on top of the other based on data order. Insert the following code into your Python script file.

```python
# -*- coding: utf-8 -*-
import pygal

#Create a new stacked bar chart.
bar = pygal.StackedBar()
bar.title = 'Searches for term: sleep'
bar.x_labels = map(str, range(2011, 2015))
bar.add('Men', [81, 88, 88, 100])
bar.add('Women', [78, 84, 69, 92])
bar.render_to_file('bar_chart.svg')
```

The following is the output of executing the script above:

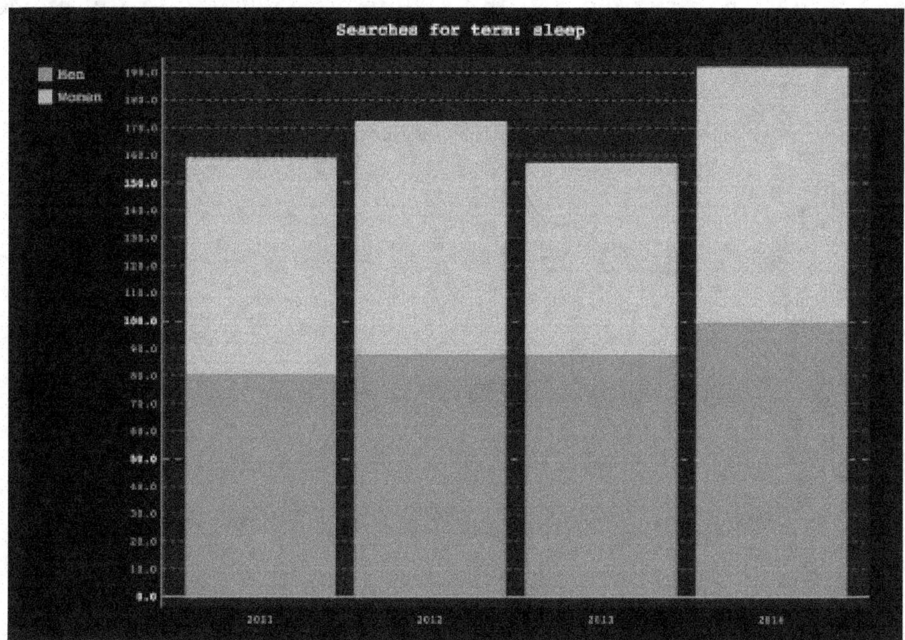

You have two pieces of data since this is a layered value. Men and women search in the following instance. The image above is a complete chart that shows the total number of searches for the word "sleep" in different parts of the data set.

Horizontal Bar Charts

This is the last bar chart that Pygal offers. You will use a horizontal chart and use the data from the last bar chart. A horizontal bar chart is designed to show data at a single moment in time.As a result, you will delete your x labels attribute since you just want to show a single month. Now, insert the following code and run the script:

```python
# -*- coding: utf-8 -*-
import pygal
#create a new bar chart.
bar = pygal.HorizontalBar()
bar.title = 'Searches for term: sleep in April'
bar.add('Searches', [81, 88, 88, 100])
bar.render_to_file('bar_chart.svg'
```

Open the bar chart.svg file and the results are indicated in the image below:

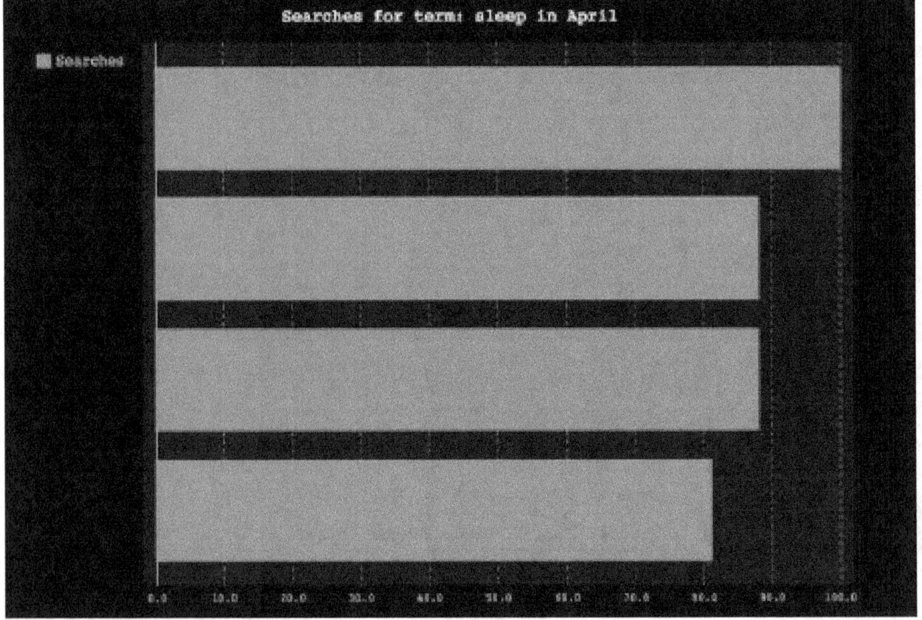

XY Charts

The XY chart is often used in scientific data to show a wide range of values over time. They may also show negative values.To improve readability, these charts may produce different sets. Now, using the code provided below, make a basic xy chart with two points.

```python
# -*- coding: utf-8 -*-
import pygal
xy_chart = pygal.XY()
xy_chart.add('Value 1', [(-50, -30), (100, 45)])
xy_chart.render_to_file("xy_chart.svg")
```

Go to the xychart.svg file. The outcomes are shown in the image below:

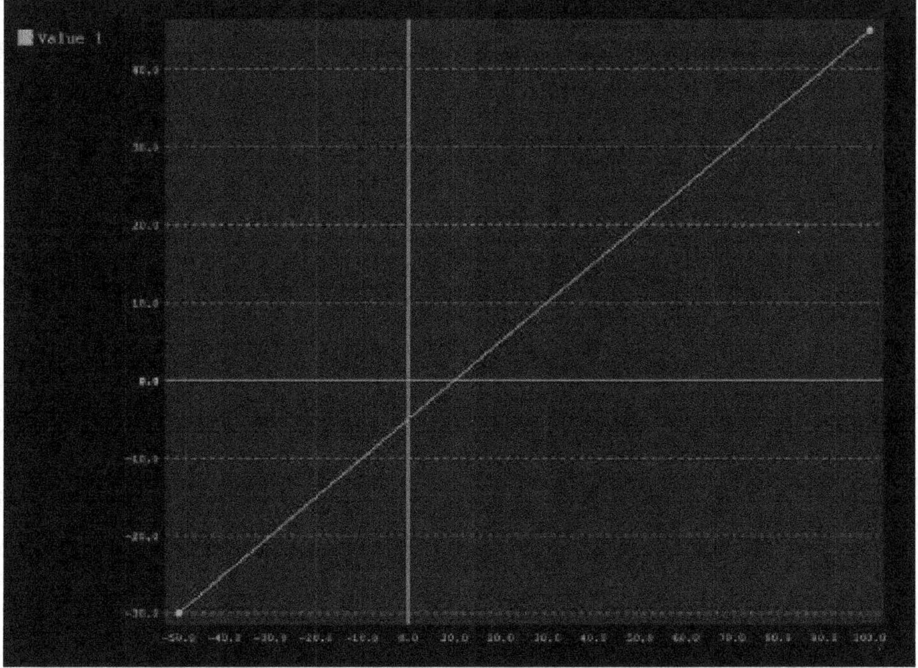

Take note of how pygal emphasizes the o lines on both the x and y coordinates. This is a freestyle to illustrate negative values that are supported by the pygal library. Take notice of the add () method, as well as how each value is emphasized as an (x. y) coordinate, categorized in an array. Let's make another chart, but this time with two plots. In the following example, we will use Value 1 and Value 2 to construct. Run the Python script after inserting the following code.

```python
# -*- coding: utf-8 -*-
import pygal
xy_chart = pygal.XY()
xy_chart.add('Value 1', [(-50, -30), (100, 45)])
xy_chart.add('Value 2', [(-2, -14), (370, 444)])
xy_chart.render_to_file("xy_chart.svg")
```

Go to the xychart.svg file. Recall that the two-line plots, as seen in the screenshot, are present:

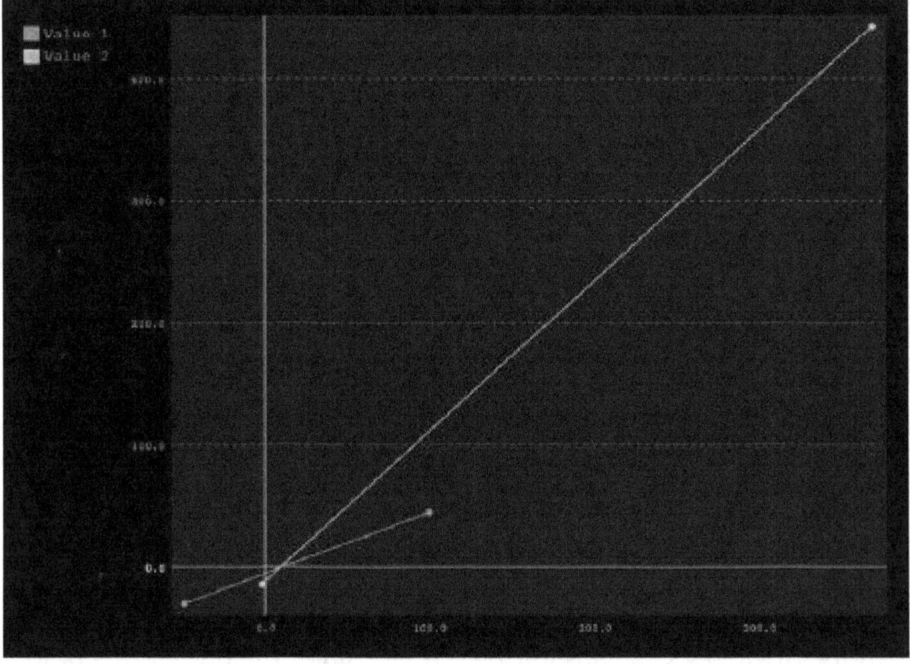

After that, you'll learn how to create a simple line plot in an XY chart, but what if you have many values in a single line? Another XY chart with three values and six dots per value will be created.Copy and execute the following code.

```python
# -*- coding: utf-8 -*-
import pygal
xy_chart = pygal.XY()
xy_chart.add('Value 1', [(-50, -30), (100, 45), (120, 56), (168,
102), (211, 192), (279, 211)])
xy_chart.add('Value 2', [(-2, -14), (370, 444), (391, 464), (399,
512), (412, 569), (789, 896)])
xy_chart.add('Value 3', [(2, 10), (142, 164), (184, 216), (203, 243),
(208, 335), (243, 201)])
xy_chart.render_to_file("xy_chart.svg")
```

After it is finished, open the xychart.svg file, which should look like the screenshot below:

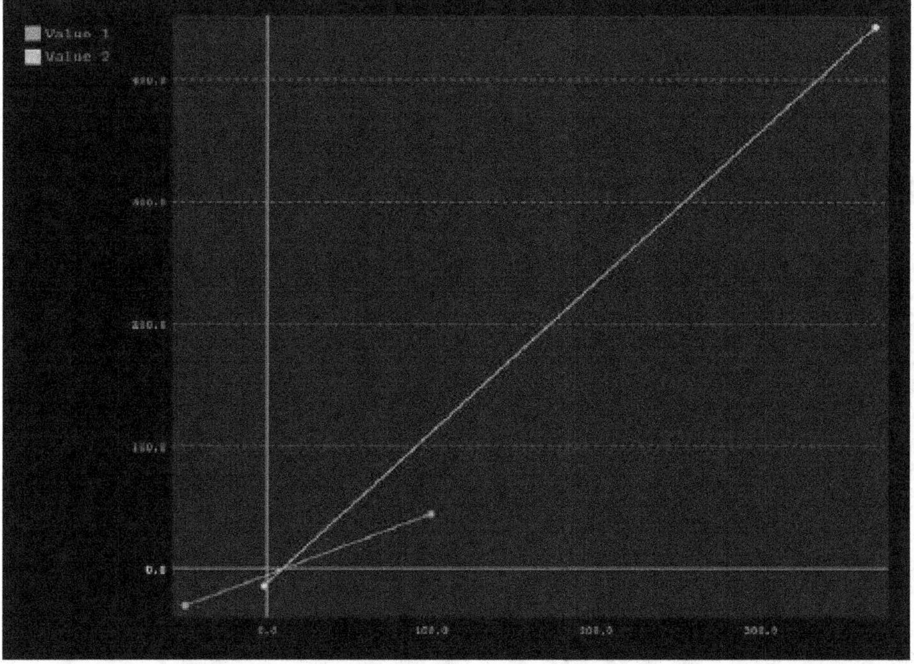

Examine how simple it is to read each dataset. Value 2 has the highest values that are on the upper side, and Value 3 has a greater point than Value 1 but swiftly drops down. As a result, XY charts are useful for scientific data. Consider scatter plots, which are a kind of XY chart.

Scatter Plots

This operates similarly to XY charts; however, there are no connecting lines. The "scatterplot" function does not exist in the pygal package. However, you repeat the XY chart function and provide a parameter. In the following example, stroke equals False. Let's duplicate the XY code from the last chart and add the stroke parameter.

```python
# -*- coding: utf-8 -*-
import pygal
xy_chart = pygal.XY(stroke=False)
xy_chart.add('Value 1', [(-50, -30), (100, 45), (120, 56), (168,
102), (211, 192), (279, 211)])
xy_chart.add('Value 2', [(-2, -14), (370, 444), (391, 464), (399,
512), (412, 569), (789, 896)])
xy_chart.add('Value 3', [(2, 10), (142, 164), (184, 216), (203, 243),
(208, 335), (243, 201)])
xy_chart.render_to_file("xy_chart.svg")
```

Run the file after you've finished copying this code. Your scatter plots should look like the one in the image below:

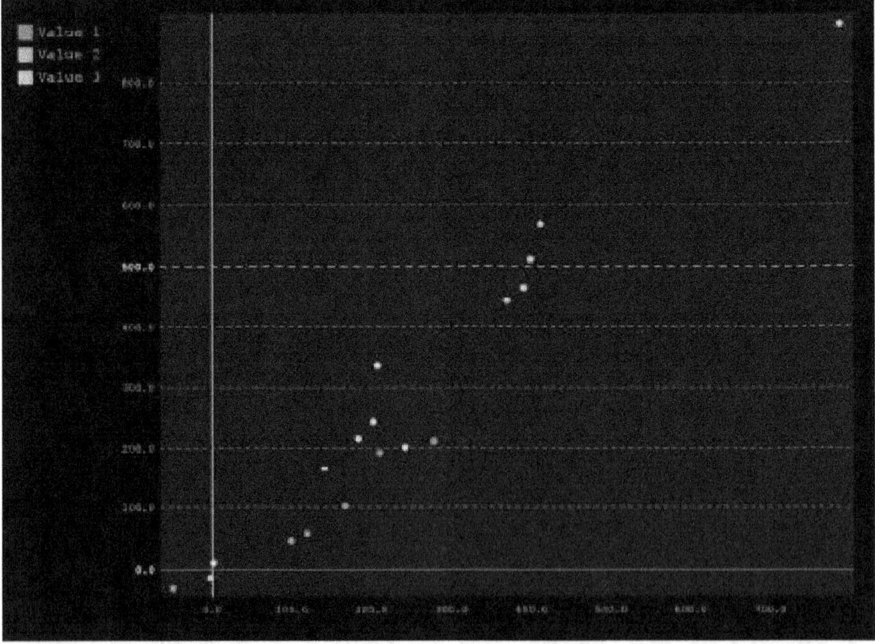

Please take note of how simple it is to read this chart with several data points. When you have more than 10 data points per dataset or more than 6 datasets to present, use XY charts instead of scatter plots.

The DateY is the last variant of the xy chart library in Pygal.

Date Y Charts

With one exception, this chart works precisely like the XY chart. In Python, each data point is linked to a date, which is shown as a real datetime object instead of a string type. Inside the Python code, each X label will be linked to a date object, and Y will be either an integer or a float given by us. Moreover, DateY has its own role with its own set of regulations to follow. Let's make a basic DateY chart to see what we're dealing with. First, examine the datetime library before implementing the following code. This library is a Python built-in library that is rather basic. It allows you to save dates and count back or ahead of time. The datetime library includes the timedelta function. Using date-based parameters, timedelta () shows the length of time between two dates or times and the difference between them.

```python
import datetime
from time import sleep
start = datetime.datetime.now()
sleep(5) #delay the python script for 5 seconds.
stop = datetime.datetime.now()
elapsed = stop - start
if elapsed > datetime.timedelta(minutes=4):
print "Slept for greater than 4 minutes"
if elapsed > datetime.timedelta(seconds=4):
print "Slept for greater than 4 seconds"
```

The output of the following code is displayed below. Note that the script uses the sleep () function to set a 5-second delay before setting the date of the stop variable.

Let's now create the DateY chart. You will need to timestamp an array of dates using values for this graphic.

```python
# -*- coding: utf-8 -*-
import pygal
from datetime import datetime, timedelta
Date_Y = pygal.DateY()
Date_Y.title = "Flights and amount of passengers arriving from St.Louis."
Date_Y.add("Arrival", [
(datetime(2014, 1, 5), 42),
(datetime(2014, 1, 14), 123),
(datetime(2014, 2, 2), 97),
(datetime(2014, 3, 22), 164)
])
Date_Y.render_to_file('datey_chart.svg')
```

Let's go through this chart again. We can see that each data point, as well as our char value, is associated with a complete date-time. On the x-axis label, you may also see a time range. Nevertheless, there is an issue with this. Examine the chart below carefully, paying particular attention to the labels on the x-axis.

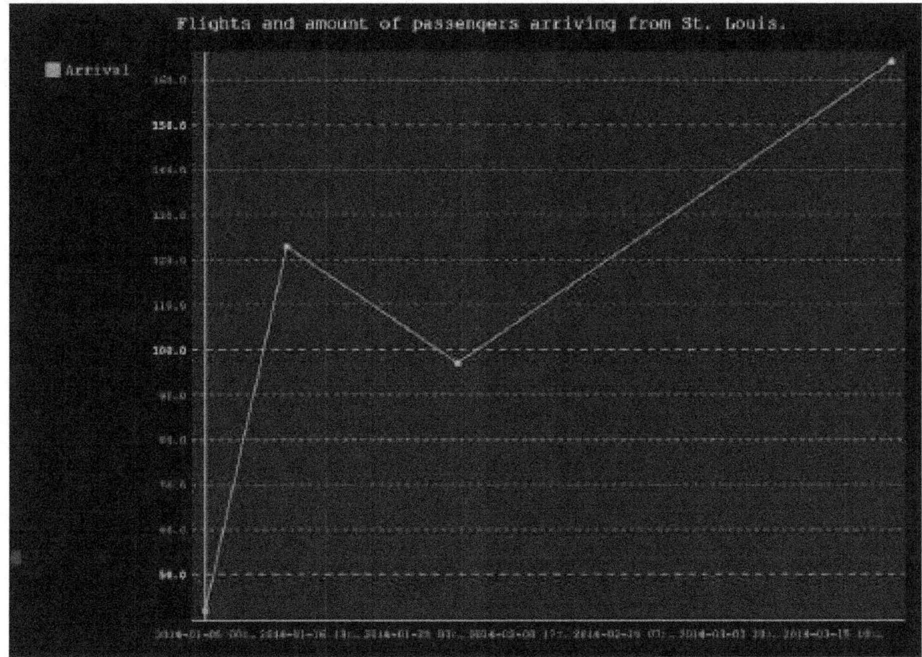

Look at how the labels cluster together and crop off if they don't fit. This should not be an issue for you since the DateY chart has an extra parameter that will let you display these labels. You may rotate them along the x-axis by using the parameter shown in the code below:

```python
# -*- coding: utf-8 -*-
import pygal
from datetime import datetime, timedelta
Date_Y = pygal.DateY(x_label_rotation=25)
Date_Y.title = "Flights and amount of passengers arriving from St.Louis."
Date_Y.add("Arrival", [
(datetime(2014, 1, 5), 42),
(datetime(2014, 1, 14), 123),
(datetime(2014, 2, 2), 97),
(datetime(2014, 3, 22), 164)
])
Date_Y.render_to_file('datey_chart.svg')
```

Re-render the chart as seen in the image below. The labels are designed in a manner that promotes reading, as you can see.

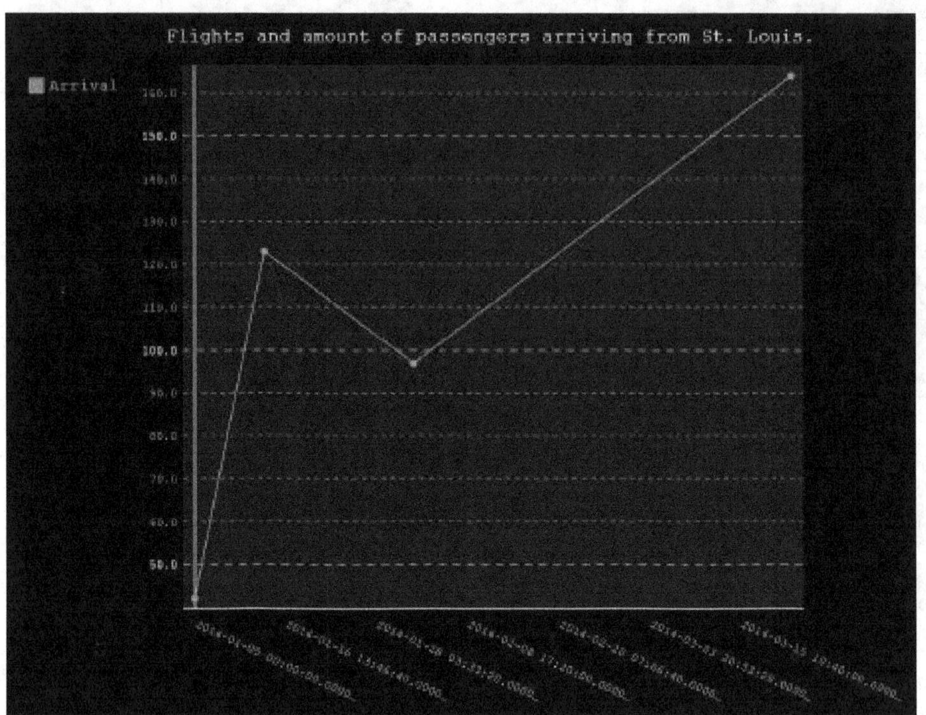

Let's add one more chart before we go on to the next chapter. In the following example, you'll record two points in time known to your code; one will be delayed using a sleep delay similar to the time delta example, and two aircraft will arrive at two separate times.

You'll select a delay between two arrivals and the time for each data point here. You will request time. To postpone the script, use sleep (). Carry out this script. Recall that since the chart's code involves a delay, the SVG file will take 277 seconds to process:

```python
# -*- coding: utf-8 -*-
import pygal, time
from datetime import datetime
#Set pre-defined arrival dates for compare.
arrival1 = datetime.now()
time.sleep(277)
arrival2 = datetime.now()
delta = arrival2 - arrival1
result = str(delta.seconds) + ' seconds'
Date_Y = pygal.DateY(x_label_rotation=25)
Date_Y.title = "Flights and amount of passengers arriving from St.Louis."
Date_Y.add("Arrival", [
(datetime(2014, 1, 5), 42),
(datetime(2014, 1, 14), 123),
(datetime(2014, 2, 2), 97),
(datetime(2014, 3, 22), 164)
])
Date_Y.add("Arrivals today (time between flights %s)" % result, [
(arrival1, 14),
(arrival2, 47)
])
Date_Y.render_to_file('datey_chart.svg')
```

Let us now look at the outcomes. While the timings aren't too far apart, you may want to mouse over for a more detailed look at how much time has passed. Our label indicates that 277 seconds have passed.

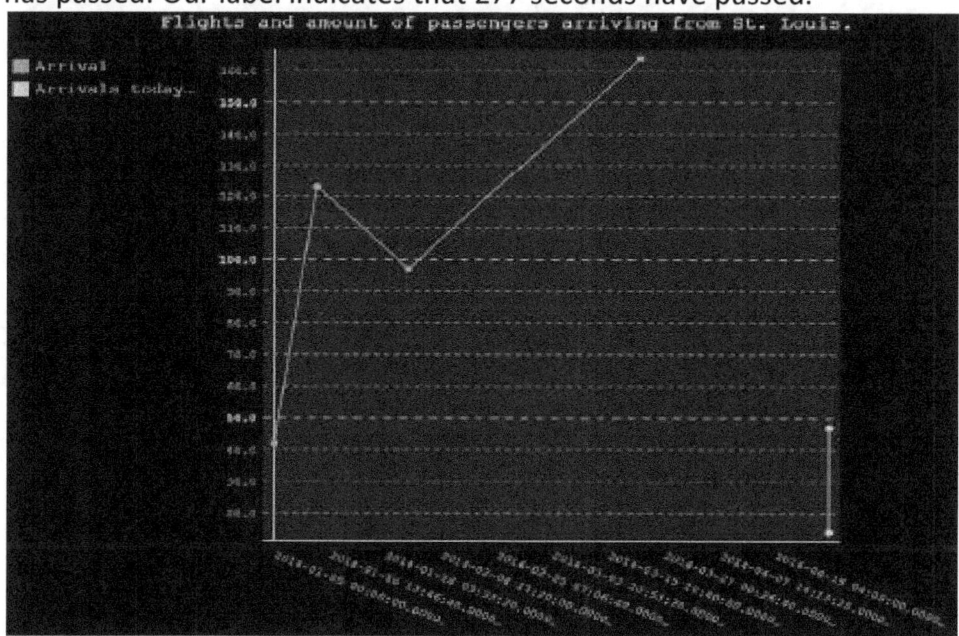

Chapter 6:

Data Analysis

nalyzing a dataset to find patterns is a skill. There may be many metrics associated with a dataset, and you want to see the needle in the following haystack. The needle in your situation is the insight you're looking for in the data that you're not aware of. In this example, understanding may relate to valuable information about consumers who buy milk from one manufacturer and cereal from another. The goods may then be arranged close to the retail shop.

When you choose to study a dataset, you must have a thorough understanding of both the dataset and the domain with which it is associated. The analysis should be done immediately if the dataset is primary and easy to understand. On the other hand, if the dataset has some similarities to turbine sensor data, knowing how turbines work and what is essential to their operation will make your study richer.

You may steer your analysis by mastering a domain.
What is Data Mining?

Data mining is the process of using machine learning, database systems, and statistics to look at data and find patterns. The end goal of data mining is to get valuable information from data, which can then be used to make more money, cut costs, or even save lives through some of its applications. When you have a dataset to mine, you can't use all of the available data-mining methods on each column field to find insights. This will be a challenging process, and any key ideas will take a long time to emerge.

Understanding domains is crucial for improving the data mining process. The following information will help you know what the data represents and how to analyze it to get insights. The best method to start data mining is to extract themes from the data that needs to be mined. If you have sales data from a Fast Moving Consumer Goods firm, the following themes might emerge:

Behavior of a brand
Outlet behavior
Product expansion
The seasonal impact on goods

The themes assist in directing data exploration and pattern discovery.
After you've identified the themes, create questions for each to help you refine your research.
As an example:

Brand etiquette: The following questions were used to supplement the analysis:

-Which brands are the best?

-Which brands have the most reach?
-Which firms are stealing other brands' sales?

The following questions can help you refine your analysis of outlet behavior.
-

What proportion of outlets use 80% of revenue?
-Which kind of stores have the most sales?
-What kinds of stores offer significant luxury products?

Product expansion: Below are the questions that were used to simplify the following subject.
-How many of your brands are seasonal?
- What is the difference between seasonal and non-seasonal sales?
-Which holiday produces the most sales for a certain brand?

The preceding questions below these topics provide specific recommendations for identifying trends and doing quality analysis.
The flow chart below summarizes the data exploration process:

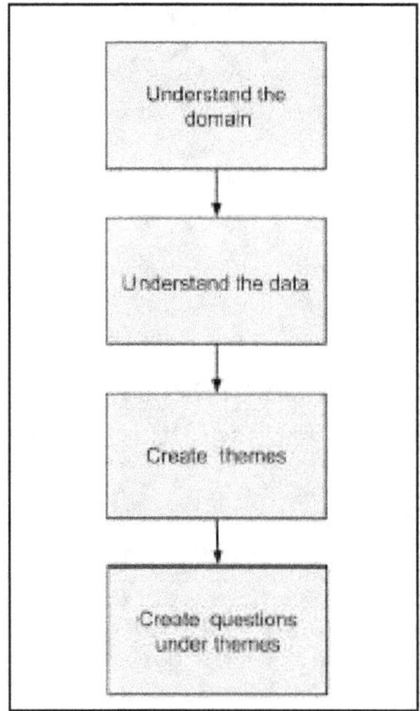

Present an Analysis

After your analysis, you should give particular observations based on your findings. The most common method is to use Microsoft PowerPoint presentations. The outcome of your research might take the shape of a chart or table. There is certain information that must be included in your presentations when presenting these constructions. This is one of the most often-used templates:

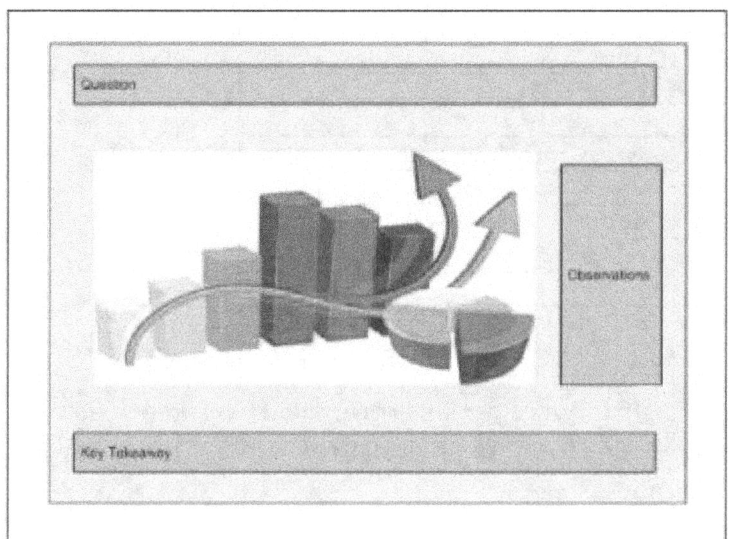

The following are the various sections of the initial image:

The uppermost component of the template should define the issue stated that a thorough analysis is attempting to concentrate on.

Observation: In this example, observations from the construct are highlighted in a vertical column. The observations may sometimes be marked with arrows.

Important takeaway: At the bottom of the graphic, explain what the chart has determined.

Exploring the Titanic

The Titanic dataset from Kaggle will be used for data analysis.

The dataset is simple to grasp and requires no domain knowledge to extract insights.

This dataset contains information on every passenger aboard the Titanic, including whether or not they survived.

The following are the field descriptions:

Field	Descriptions
survival	Survival(0 = No, 1 = Yes)
pclass	Passenger class(1 = 1st, 2 = 2nd, 3 = 3rd)
name	Name of the passenger
sex	Gender of the passenger
age	Age of the passenger
sibsp	Number of siblings/spouses aboard
parch	Number of parents/children aboard
ticket	Ticket number
fare	Passenger fare
cabin	Cabin
embarked	Port of embarkation (C = Cherbourg, Q = Queenstown, S = Southampton)

Since the data is straightforward to interpret, you will keep survival analysis as the primary focus for data analysis. You'll insert the following questions around the themes:

Some of the questions to which you will reply are as follows:

Which category of travelers has the most survivors?
What is the proportion of non-survivors among classes on the ship with relatives?
What is the gender distribution of the survivors among the different classes?
What is the survival rate for different age groups?
Which class of passengers has the highest number ofsurvivors?

To answer this question, you will make a basic bar plot showing the number of survivors and the percentage of survival in each class.

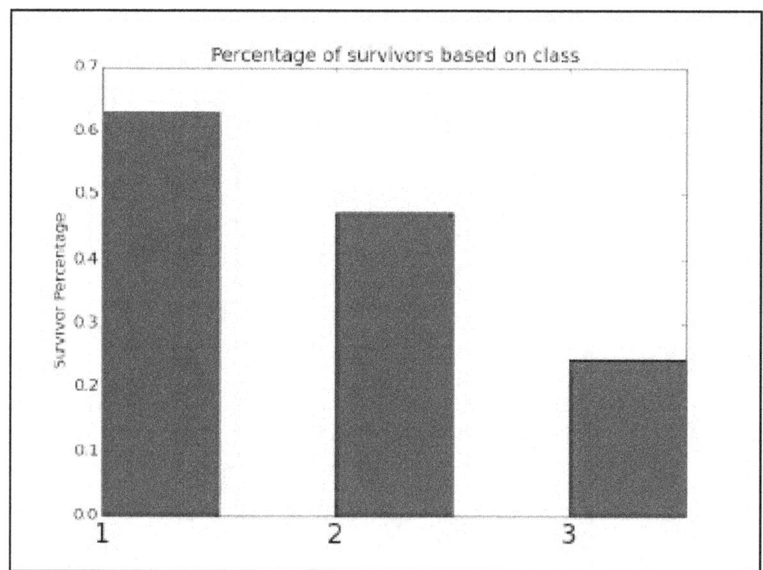

You must do a preliminary check for null values on the fields that are used in your code. Next, for each class, determine the number of survivors and the percentage of survivors. Next, create two bar charts to determine the total number of survivors and the percentage of survivors.

These are your thoughts:

The first and third classes have the largest number of survivors, respectively.

In terms of the total number of passengers in each class, the first class has the greatest survival rate, at roughly 61%.

In terms of the total number of passengers in each class, the third class has the largest number of survivors, almost 25%.
Now for the main point:

When the ship was sinking, there was clearly a preference for rescuing people in first class. It also had the greatest proportion of survivors.
What is the gender distribution of survivors across various classes? Men and women in their respective classes.

The solution to this question is that you will use this code to create a side-by-side bar chart to compare the various rates and percentages among m.

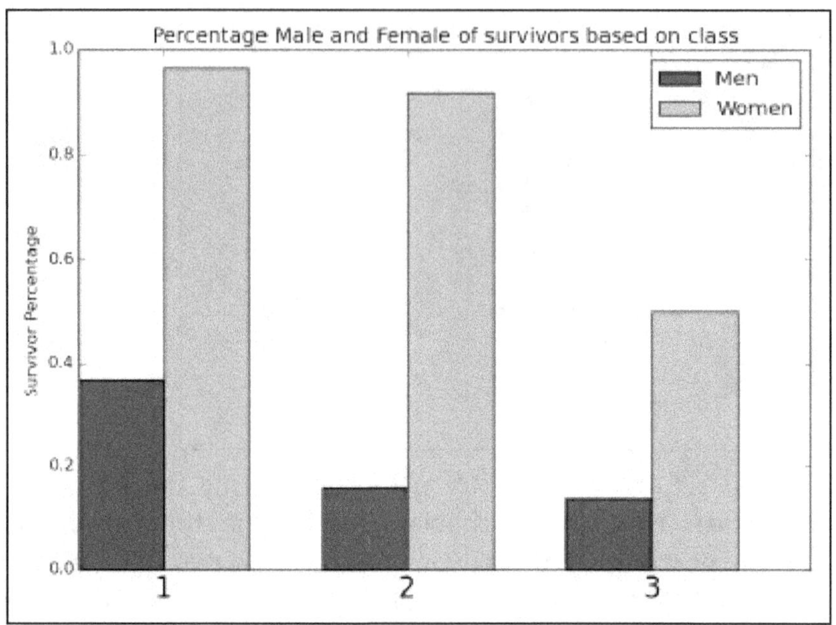

The number of male and female survivors is calculated, and a side-by-side bar plot is created. After that, the proportion of male and female survival in relation to the total number of men and females in their respective classes is calculated and shown.

These are our findings:
The majority of survivors are girls across all grades.
More than 90% of first and second-class female passengers survived.
The survival rates of male passengers in first and third class are similar.

The Most Important Thing

Female passengers were given priority for lifeboats, and the vast majority were rescued.

What is the distribution of non-survivors among the different
classes who have family aboard the ship?

To solve this question, you will build code to plot bar charts using the total number of non-survivors in each class who had family onboard, as well as the proportion of total passengers. Your code will be similar to that used in the previous questions. In this situation, you may calculate the number of non-survivors with families and then do the standard bar graphs.

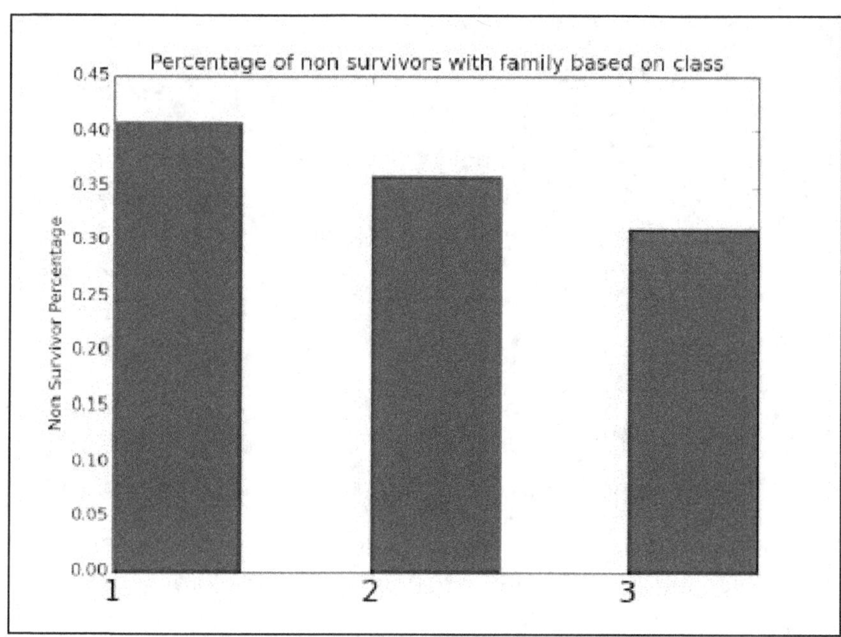

These are some conclusions you may draw:

In the third class, there are numerous non-survivors.

The second class has the fewest non-survivors who have relatives.

In terms of overall passengers, the first class, which includes family, has the most non-survivors, while the third class has the fewest.

While the third class had the most number of non-survivors with family onboard, it primarily contained passengers who did not have relatives aboard. In contrast, the first class had the greatest number of passengers with relatives aboard.

What is the survival percentage among various age groups?

For this question, you will develop the following code to generate pie charts that compare the proportion of survivors depending on the number and percentage of survivors in each age group:

```python
>>> #Checking for null values
>>> df['Age'].isnull().value_counts()
>>> False 714
>>> True 177
>>> dtype: int64
>>> #Defining the age binning interval
>>> age_bin = [0, 18, 25, 40, 60, 100]
>>> #Creating the bins
>>> df['AgeBin'] = pd.cut(df.Age, bins=age_bin)
>>> #Removing the null rows
>>> d_temp = df[np.isfinite(df['Age'])] # removing all na instances
>>> #Number of survivors based on Age bin
>>> survivors = d_temp.groupby('AgeBin')['Survived'].agg(sum)
>>> #Total passengers in each bin
>>> total_passengers = d_temp.groupby('AgeBin')['Survived'].agg('count')
>>> #Plotting the pie chart of total passengers in each bin
>>> plt.pie(total_passengers,
labels=total_passengers.index.values.tolist(),
autopct='%1.1f%%', shadow=True, startangle=90)
>>> plt.title('Total Passengers in different age groups')
>>> plt.show()
```

In the following code, you set the bin by using the age bin variable and adding a column called AgeBin. The cut function fills the bin values in the AgeBin column. After that, you filter out all the rows with the age set to null. Next, you make two pie charts, one for the total number of passengers in each age group and the other for the total number of survivors in each age group.

The following are my observations:

The 25-40 age group has the most passengers, while the 0-18 age group has the second most passengers.

The 18-25 age group had the second-highest number of survivors among those who survived.

The age range 60-100 has the lowest percentage of survival.

The 25-40 age group had the most survival compared to any other age group, while the elderly were either unlucky or made way for the younger people to board the lifeboats.

This chapter has looked at the definition of data mining. You've learned how to use data mining in a methodical way and how important it is to know about the subject area. You've also learned about the many methods to communicate data mining findings.

Chapter 7:

Explore Machine Learning

Machine Learning is a method of teaching programs that develop algorithms from data rather than explicitly programming an algorithm from the beginning. This is a branch of computer science that stems from artificial intelligence research. It is strongly connected to statistics and mathematical optimization, which offer the discipline tools, application fields, and theories. Machine learning is used in a variety of computer jobs when programming is impractical.

Email spam filters, language translation, search engines, and computer versions are all examples of applications. Machine learning is often mistaken for data mining, despite the fact that it focuses primarily on exploratory data analysis.

The following terminology will be used in the next chapter:

Features: These are distinct characteristics that will assist in determining the outcome.

Sample: A sample is an object that must be processed. It might be a paper, an audio file, a picture, or a CSV file.
Feature Vector: A numerical feature, such as an n-dimensional vector, that represents an item.
Feature extraction: This is the process of converting data from a high-dimensional space to a lower-dimensional one using a feature vector.
A training set is a collection of data that is used to uncover highly predictive correlations.
A testing set is a collection of data that is used to make predictions.

Various Types of Machine Learning
Depending on the nature of the learning objective or the feedback provided to the learning system, machine learning is classified into three types:

Supervised Learning: A set of inputs and outputs are assigned to the computer. The program's purpose is to learn from the inputs and duplicate the outcomes.
Learning without supervision. In the case of unsupervised learning, there is no goal variable. The computer is left alone to find patterns in the data.
Reinforcement learning is the third kind of learning. Software, like driving a vehicle, must interact with its surroundings in a dynamic manner.

Supervised Learning

As previously stated, a supervised learning algorithm masters the training data and provides a function that can be used to predict future occurrences.

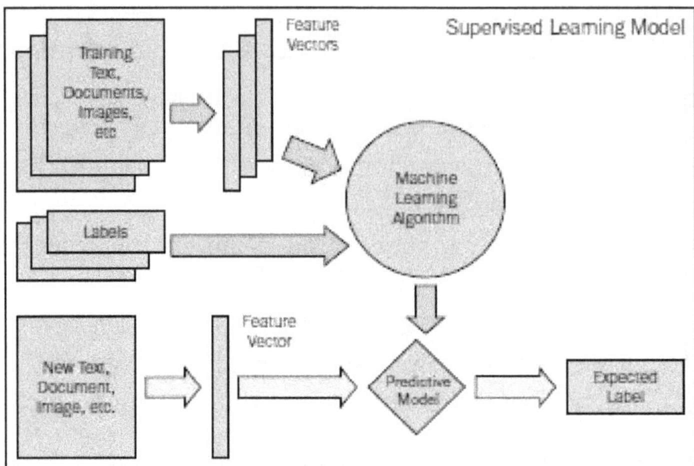

As seen in the preceding figure, there is training data from which the machine learning model will learn.

Assume that the training data comprises a collection of text that reflects various news items. These news stories are relevant to sports, national, international, and other news categories. These types of news will serve as labels. You will extract feature vectors from the following training data, where each word may be a vector or retrieved from the text. For example, the number of times the term "Football" appears may be a vector, as can the number of times the phrase "Prime Minister" appears. These feature vectors and labels are sent into the machine learning algorithm, which uses the data to learn. After training, the model is applied to new data, where the characteristics are retrieved and entered into the model, which outputs the target data.

Here are some examples of supervised machine learning algorithms, which you will explore briefly in the next chapter and in more detail in subsequent chapters.

Decision trees

Logistic regression

Linear regression

The naïve Bayes classifier

Unsupervised Learning

Unsupervised learning, as previously said, seeks to uncover latent structures in unlabeled data. There is no label put into the algorithm in the figure below.

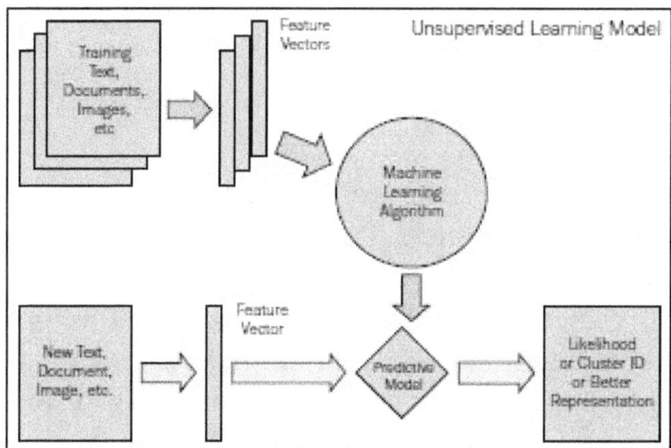

Consider the photographs that will serve as the input training dataset. The illustrations depict human, insect, and horse faces. Features are obtained from these photographs, which aid in determining the group to which the images belong. The unsupervised machine learning method is then enhanced with these characteristics. The program will find patterns in the data and aid in assigning photographs to the appropriate category.

This similar technique may then be used to fresh photos to help in bucketing them into the appropriate categories.

The examples below are of unsupervised machine learning methods, which will be discussed in the next chapter.

The k-means clustering algorithm
Clustering based on hierarchies

Reinforcement Learning

In reinforcement learning, the data to be entered serves as a stimulus to the model from the environment, to which the machine learning model must respond. Feedback is created in the background rather than as a teaching procedure, as in the case of supervised learning.

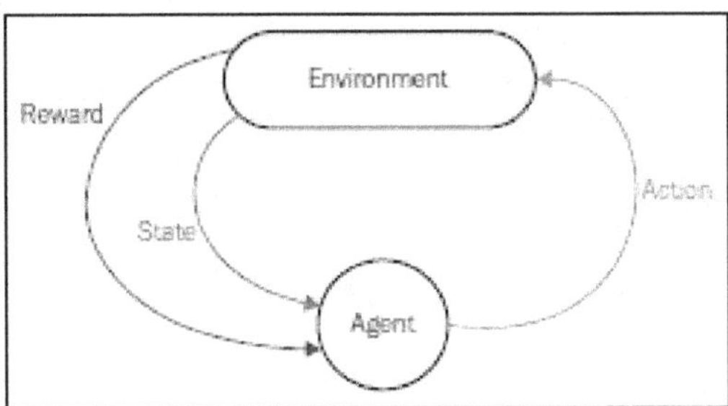

Learning occurs as a consequence of the agent's actions. Rather than being formally taught, the effort it picks is dependent on its prior experience as well as new options made by it, implying that it learns by trial and error. The agent receives the reinforcement signal in the form of a numerical reward that encodes success, and the agent attempts to educate itself to do behaviors that will increase the cumulative reward over time.

Reinforcement learning is widely used in robots but not in data science. The following are reinforcement learning algorithms:

Q education
Learning from temporal differences

Decision Trees
A basic predictive model relates an item's outputs to the input data. It is a well-known predictive modeling approach that is widely used in business.
There are two kinds of decision tree models:

Classifier trees: They direct attention to dependent variables with finite values. The branches of these tree structures indicate the rules of the characteristics that result in class labels, and the leaves represent the class labels of the outcomes.

Regression trees: Regression trees are used when dependent variables accept continuous values.

Consider the following example. The following information decides whether or not you should play tennis based on the overall look of the weather, wind strength, and humidity.

Play	Wind	Humidity	Outlook
No	Low	High	Sunny
No	High	Normal	Rain
Yes	Low	High	Overcast
Yes	Weak	Normal	Rain
Yes	Low	Normal	Sunny
Yes	Low	Normal	Overcast
Yes	High	Normal	Sunny

If you take the following data and apply Play as the goal variable and the remainder as the independent variable, you will obtain a decision tree model with the following structure as the rules:

As a consequence, when fresh data is received, this tree will be reversed to provide the following outcome:

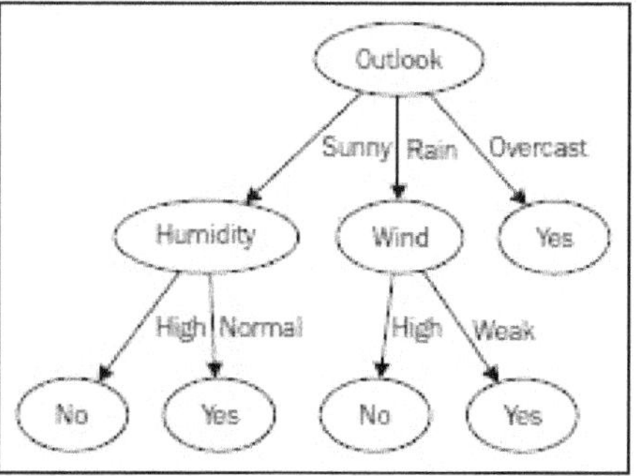

Decision trees are the most straightforward prediction models, and here are some of their benefits:

Decision trees are simple to express and depict.

Old patterns may be discovered. Assume you want to determine the voting trend between two parties for an election, and you have data on education, sex, age, and income. You may see a trend in which highly educated individuals have relatively low incomes and vote for a certain party.

Decision trees have the fewest data assumptions.

The downsides of a decision tree are listed below.

There is a high classification error rate, despite the fact that the training set is minimal in comparison to the number of classes.

As the data and the number of dependent variables grow in big, there is an exponential expansion in determining.

A discrete data set is required for a certain building procedure.

Linear Regression

Linear regression is a modeling technique that establishes a scalar linear connection between a scalar dependent variable and an independent variable, X, which may have one or more values:

$$y = X\beta + \varepsilon$$

Let me provide an example to demonstrate this. This table shows the height and weight of each student in a class:

Height (inches)	Weight (pounds)
50	125
58	135
63	145
68	144
70	170
79	165
84	171
75	166
65	160

If we run the following using a basic linear regression function with weight as the dependent variable, y, and height as the independent variable, x, we obtain the following equation:

$$y = 1.405405405\,x + 57.87687688$$

If you display the above equation as a line with 57.88 as the intercept and 1.4 cm as the slope on top of a scatter plot with Weight on the y-axis and Height on the x-axis, you will obtain the following plot:

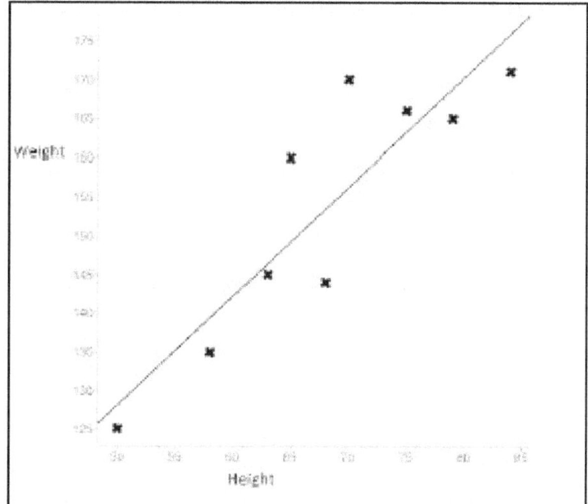

In the above example, the regression method seeks to construct the preceding equation with the least amount of error when predicting the student's weight. This is a basic linear regression example.

Logistic Regression

Logistic regression, which is a probabilistic classification model, is another supervised learning strategy. It is often used to predict a binary predictor, such as whether or not a credit card transaction is fraudulent. Logistics is used in logistic regression. A logistic function is a useful function that can take any number between 0 and infinity and return values between 0 and 1. As a result, it might be interpreted as a likelihood. This is a logistic function that predicts values ranging from o to 1 based on the x variable:

$$F(x) = \frac{1}{1 + e^{-(\beta_0 + \beta_1 x)}}$$

In the above example, x is the independent variable, and F(x) is the dependent variable.

If you plot the logistic function from negative infinity to positive infinity, you will get the S-shaped graph shown below:

Logistic regression may be used in the following situations:
Refusing to provide a propensity score to a consumer at a retail shop for likelihood of a transformer failing to function

The likelihood of a person clicking on an ad presented on a website based on their activity.

Logistic regression has several applications, which will be discussed in detail in the following chapters.

The Nave Bayes Classifier is a kind of classification algorithm.
The naive Bayes classifier is a straightforward probabilistic classifier based on the Bayes theorem. The assumption here is that the characteristics are highly interdependent; as a consequence, it is said to as naive. The Bayes theorem is as follows:

$$P(A\mid B) = \frac{P(B\mid A)P(A)}{P(B)}$$

A and B are occurrences in the preceding formula, and p(A) and p(B) are the probability of A and B. Moreover, they depend on one another. P(A|B) denotes the probability of A if B is True, which is a conditional probability. P (B|A) is the probability of B if A is True. The following is the naive Bayes formula:

$$P(A_k\mid B) = P(A_k \cap B)/P(A_1 \cap B) + P(A_2 \cap B) + \ldots + P(A_n \cap B)$$

Let us attempt to solve the above naive Bayes formula using the following example:

Ann will be attending an outdoor event in Austin tomorrow. In recent years, Austin has only had six rainy days in a year. Regrettably, the weatherman has predicted rain for tomorrow. The weatherman correctly forecasted rain 80% of the time. Nonetheless, he anticipates the weather wrong 20% of the time when it does not rain. Determine the chance that it will rain on Ann's wedding day. Some of the circumstances on which the probability may be calculated are as follows:

A1. According to this occurrence, it rains on Ann's engagement.
A2. This occurrence says that it will not rain at Ann's wedding.
B. According to this incident, the weatherman predicts rain.
The following are the probability based on prior occurrences.

P(AI) = 6/365. To put it another way, it rains six days a year.
P(AII)=359/365. In other words, it does not rain 359 days a year.
P (B| AI). In other words, it rains as predicted by the weatherman 80% of the time.

P (B| AII). This indicates that it does not rain as forecast by the weatherman 20% of the time.

This formula ensures that the naive Bayes probability is computed:

$$P(AI \mid B) = P(AI)P(B \mid AI)/(P(AI)P(B \mid AI) + P(AII)P(B \mid AII))$$

$$P(AI \mid B) = (0.0164 * 0.8)/(0.0164*0.8 + 0.9834 * 0.2)$$

$$P(AI \mid B) = 0.065$$

As a result of the foregoing analysis, even though the weatherman predicted rain, there is only a 6.5% chance that it would rain according to

Bayes theorem.
The naive Bayes algorithm is often used in e-mail filtering. It needs the occurrence of each term in an e-mail and assesses the chance of spam or not. The naive Bayes model learns from prior e-mail data and identifies emails as spam, which is vital in determining whether an e-mail is a spam or not.

The K-means Clustering

The k-means clustering approach is an unsupervised learning technique used to divide data from n observations into k bins of the same observations.

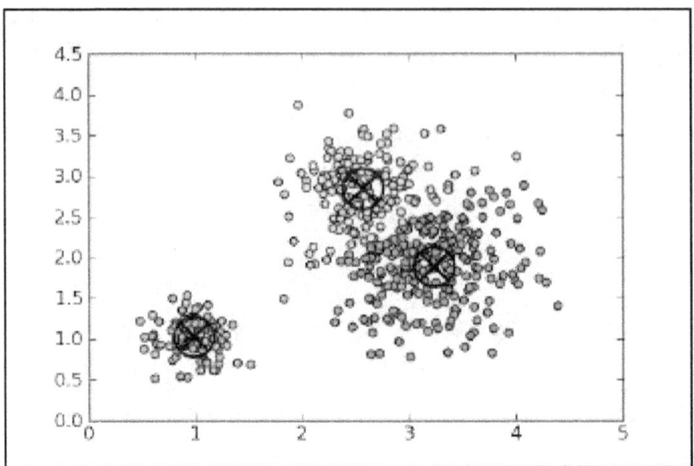

13

calculating the mean of the feature, which reflects the dependent variables you cluster, such as customer categorization based on an average transaction amount and the average number of items bought in a quarter of a year. The average value becomes the cluster's center.

The number k denotes the number of clusters. In other words, the approach entails computing a k number of means, which results in data clustering around these k-means.

How Do We Choose This K?

If you know what you're looking for or how many clusters you'll need, you may set K to that amount before starting the engines and letting the algorithm do its thing.

If you don't know the number, your investigation will take a little longer and will include some trial and error. Try k=3, 4, and 5 until you see that the clusters make sense in terms of the domain.

$$J(V) = \sum_{i=1}^{c} \sum_{j=1}^{c_i} \left(\left\| x_i - v_j \right\| \right)^2$$

|x1-v1| shows the Euclidean distance between xi and vj, c1 is the number of data points in the ith cluster, and c is the number of clusters in total.

The K-means clustering algorithm is often used in computer vision, geostatistics, and agriculture.

Later, real-world examples will be used to explain k-means clustering. Hierarchical clustering

Hierarchical clustering is an unsupervised learning strategy that generates a hierarchy of groupings from data.

This clustering captures information at many levels of a cluster tree. It is not a single collection of clusters but a multi-level hierarchy in which clusters at one level are linked to clusters at the next level. This allows you to choose the most appropriate level of grouping.

There are two kinds of hierarchical clusters:

Hierarchical agglomerative clustering. This is a bottom-up strategy in which each observation starts in its own cluster and then moves up the hierarchy via two other clusters.

Hierarchical dividing clustering. This is a top-down strategy in which observations start in a single cluster and then divide into two as they go down a hierarchy.

The following image depicts Agglomerative and Divisive hierarchical clustering:

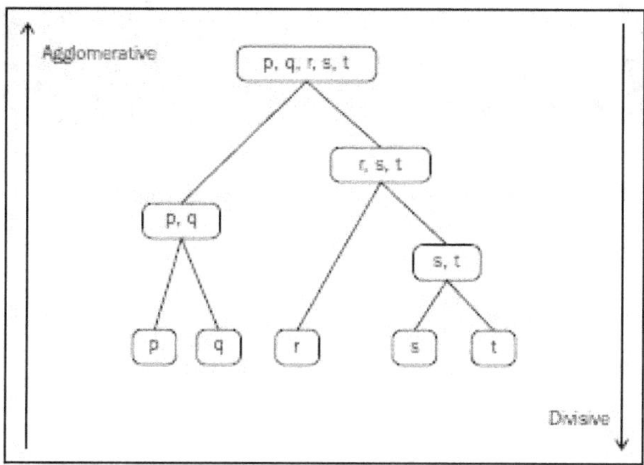

Hierarchical clustering will be thoroughly discussed.

Chapter 8:

Deep Dive- Machine Learning

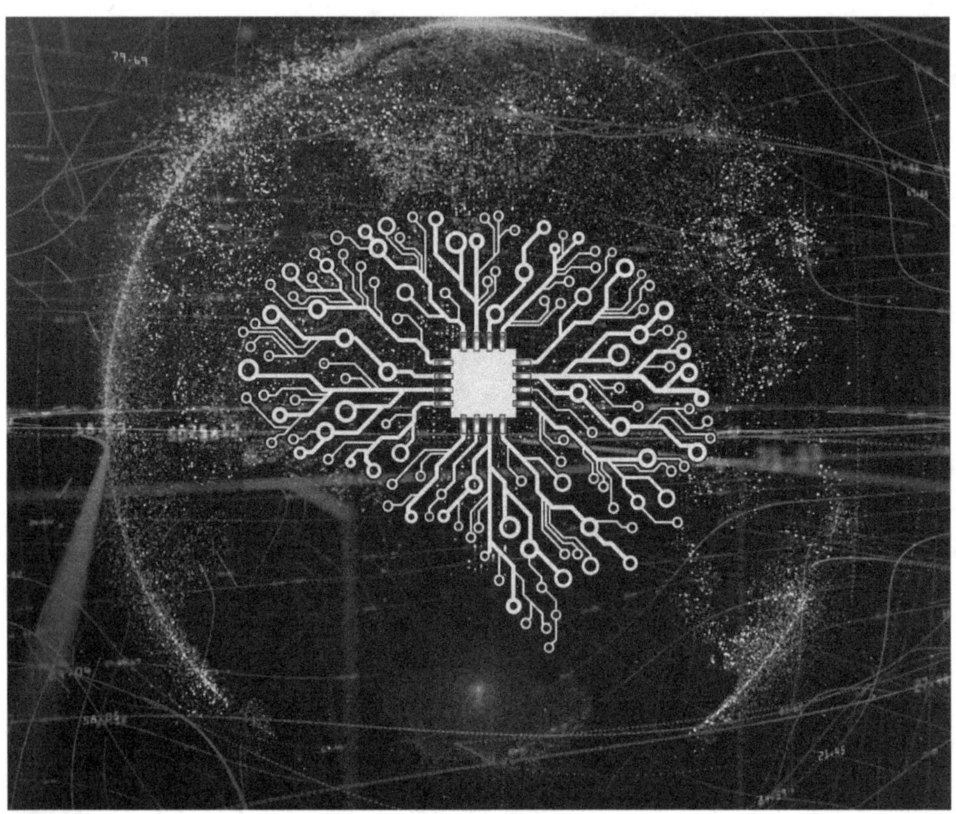

This section will focus on supervised learning methods. Every record or instance may be expressed as a set (X, Y), where X is a collection of features and y is a class label.

The goal of a classification algorithm is to master a target function, F, that maps each record's property set to one of the predetermined class labels,

A classification algorithm's usual stages are as follows:

Determine the best algorithm.

Use a training set to teach a model, and then use a test set to make sure it works.

Employ the model to forecast any previously unknown incident or record.

The first step is to choose the appropriate categorization algorithm.There is no set process for picking the optimal algorithm; it is discovered via trial and error. After the method is chosen, a training and test set is created and provided to the algorithm to train a model, that is, a target function F. A test set is used to validate the model after it has been built using a training set. In general, a confusion matrix is used to determine the model. When it comes to finding the closest neighbors, you will learn more about confusion matrices.

You will begin with a technique for dividing the input dataset into training and test sets. This will be followed by a lazy learner classification technique known as the K-Nearest neighbor.Prior to using Nave Bayes classifiers. The algorithm used in this section was not chosen at random. All of the tree algorithms covered in the next chapter can handle both multiclass and binary situations. There are more than two class labels to which the instances belong in multiclass issues.

Preparing Data for Model Creation

In the next part, you will learn how to use a dataset to generate a train and a test data set for the classification issue. The model does not present a test dataset. In practice, you would construct another dataset known as a dev. Dev stands for dataset development: a dataset that may be used to constantly adjust the model throughout subsequent runs. The model is trained using a train set, and model performance metrics like accuracy are assessed in dev. The model is further changed if adjustments are required based on the following outcome.

You will use the Iris dataset in this instance. The following dataset makes it simple to demonstrate the concept.

```python
# Load the necesssary Library
from sklearn.cross_validation import
train_test_split
from sklearn.datasets import load_iris
import numpy as np
def get_iris_data():
    """

    Returns Iris dataset
    """

    # Load iris dataset
    data = load_iris()
    # Extract the dependend and
    independent variables
    # y is our class label
    # x is our instances/records
    x = data['data']
    y = data['target']
    # For ease we merge them
    # column merge
    input_dataset = np.column_stack([x,y])
    # Let us shuffle the dataset
    # We want records distributed randomly
    # between our test and train set
    np.random.shuffle(input_dataset)
    return input_dataset
    # We need 80/20 split.
    # 80% of our records for Training
    # 20% Remaining for our Test set
    train_size = 0.8
    test_size = 1-train_size
```

```python
# get the data
input_dataset = get_iris_data()
# Split the data
train,test =
train_test_split(input_dataset,test_size=t
est_size)
# Print the size of original dataset
print "Dataset size ",input_dataset.shape
# Print the train/test split
print "Train size ",train.shape
print "Test size",test.shape
```

This was straightforward.
How it Operates

After importing the necessary library modules, you must create a useful function and call get iris data (), which will produce the Iris dataset. The x and y arrays are then concatenated into a single array called the input dataset. Then, shuffle the dataset such that the records are distributed randomly to the test and train datasets. The method returns a single array containing both instances and class labels.

If you wish to include 80% of the records in the training dataset and the remainder as the dataset. Both the train size and test size variables contain a proportion of the values in the testing and training datasets.

Use the get iris data () method to accept the supplied data.The train test split function from scikitlearn's cross-validation model may then be used to split the input dataset in half.Finally, you can see the size of the original dataset, as well as the test and train datasets.

```
Compare Data Set Size
-------------------------

Original Dataset size  (150, 5)
Train size  (120, 5)
Test  size (30, 5)
```

As you can see, the training set has received 80 percent of the 150 rows, or 120 records. You've shown how simple it is to partition input data into train and test sets.Keep in mind that this is a categorization problem. The algorithm needs to be trained so that it can guess the right class label for a case it doesn't know about. You must show the method as well as equal distribution of all classes throughout training. The Iris dataset contains three classes of problems. You must have equal representation from each of the three classes. Let's see whether the procedure has taken care of this.

It is critical to building a method called get class distribution, which chooses an array of class labels from a single y input. This function returns a dictionary with the key representing the class label, and the value is the proportion of records in this distribution. As a result, the distribution of class labels is defined by the dictionary below. To determine the class distribution on the train and test datasets, use this function in the following code.

The print class labe split method is simple. You must pass the training and test datasets as arguments. Since you concatenated x and y, the final column is our traditional label. The train and test class labels are then extracted in the y train and y test. You then provide them to get class distribution to get a dictionary containing the class labels and their distribution, which you then print.

You can then run print class label split, and the result should look like this:

```
Train data set class label distribution
==========================================

Class label =0, percentage records =0.36
Class label =1, percentage records =0.32
Class label =2, percentage records =0.33

Test data set class label distribution
==========================================

Class label =0, percentage records =0.23
Class label =1, percentage records =0.40
Class label =2, percentage records =0.37
```

Let us now calculate the result. As can be seen, the training datasets have a different distribution of class labels than the test set datasets.

In the last part of the code, you utilize scikit-stratifiedshufflesplit learn to achieve equal class distribution in the training and test sets. Let's have a look at the StratifiedShuffleSplit parameters:

```
stratified_split =
StratifiedShuffleSplit(input_dataset[:,-1]
,test_size=test_size,n_iter=1)
```

The input dataset is described in the first parameter. You pass all of the rows as well as the last column. The test size variable, which was first defined, represents the test size. With the n iter variable, you may assume that you only require one split. The print class label split function is then used to show the class label dispersion. Let's look at the output:

```
Train data set class label distribution
------------------------------------------

Class label =0, percentage records =0.33
Class label =1, percentage records =0.33
Class label =2, percentage records =0.33

Test data set class label distribution
------------------------------------------

Class label =0, percentage records =0.33
Class label =1, percentage records =0.33
Class label =2, percentage records =0.33
```

You now have the class labels spread evenly throughout the test and train sets.

There's still more...

Before using the machine learning method, you must adequately prepare the data. A consistent class distribution in both the train and test sets is required for the creation of a successful classification model. When it comes to real machine learning scenarios, you create a separate dataset known as the dev set in addition to the train and test sets. You may not get your model correct on the first try. But, you don't want to give the test dataset to the model since this may introduce bias into the next model-building cycle.

As a result, you construct this dev set that you may use while you cycle through the model-building process.

The 80/20 rule is a fantastic situation. Yet, in most actual conditions, you may not have enough data to exclude that many cases from a test group. In such instances, a variety of practical strategies are used.

Identifying the Nearest Neighbors

Before we get started, let's learn how to check to see whether the categorization model is operating properly. We mentioned the confusion matrix at one point in the chapter.

A confusion matrix is a table that shows how the actual and expected class tables are set up. Assume you have a two-class situation in which your y may take either value, T or F. Let's pretend you've trained a classifier to predict your y. You used your model to forecast the value of y. Then you may finish your confusion matrices as follows:

		Predicted	
		T	F
Actual	T	TP	FN
	F	FP	TN

It is critical to include the test set results in the table above.Remember that you are familiar with the class labels in the test set, so you can compare the classification model output to the actual class label.

Underneath TP, which stands for True Positive, is a count of all the records in the test set with labels that include T and where the model predicts T.
Underneath the FN, which stands for False Negative, is a count of all the records whose real label is T, but the algorithm predicts N.
The FP, which stands for False Positive, is a count of all the records whose actual label is F, but the method indicates T.
The acronym TN stands for True Negative, and the algorithm predicted that both the label and the original class label would be F.

Using the information about the confusion matrix that was given above, you can figure out how well our classification model works.
Accuracy is defined as the proportion of accurate forecasts to total predictions. You know from the confusion matrix that the sum of TP and TN equals the number of correct guesses.
Normally, accuracy from the training set is highly optimistic. To figure out how well the model really works, someone must look at the accuracy value of the test set.

Using this information, the first classification problem you will look into is the KNN, or "k-nearest neighbor." Before getting into the details of KNN, you should look at the rote classifier method, which is a simple way to sort things. The note classifier memorizes all of the training data; it loads all of the data into memory. It would help if you did classification on an unknown fresh training instance. It will attempt to create the new training instance using any of the existing training instances in memory. Each attribute in the training instance will be matched. If it finds a match, it forecasts the test insurance's class label as the class label of the matching training instance.

So far, you should know that this classifier will fail if the test case is not like any of the training cases that are already in memory.

KNN is similar to the rote classifier in that it searches for a similarity measure rather than an exact match. KNN, like the rote classifier, stores all of the training sets in memory. When a test instance has to be classified, it calculates the distance between the test instance and all of the training examples. It finds K's nearest occurrences inside the training set using the above space. The number of classes of the K closest neighbors is then used to make a prediction for the test set.

For example, if you have a two-class classification issue and set the K value to three, and the test record's three closest neighbors have the classes 1, 1, and 0, the test instance will be classified as 1, which is the most popular.

KNN is a member of the instance-based learning algorithm family. Moreover, the choice to classify a test case is made last; this is known as the "lazy learner."

You will produce some data for this algorithm by using SciKit's make classification function. This results in a matrix with four columns and 100 instances:

Internally, the get data function asks the make classification function to provide test data for any classification job.

It's usually a good idea to display the data before feeding it into any algorithm. The plot data function creates a scatter plot of all variables.

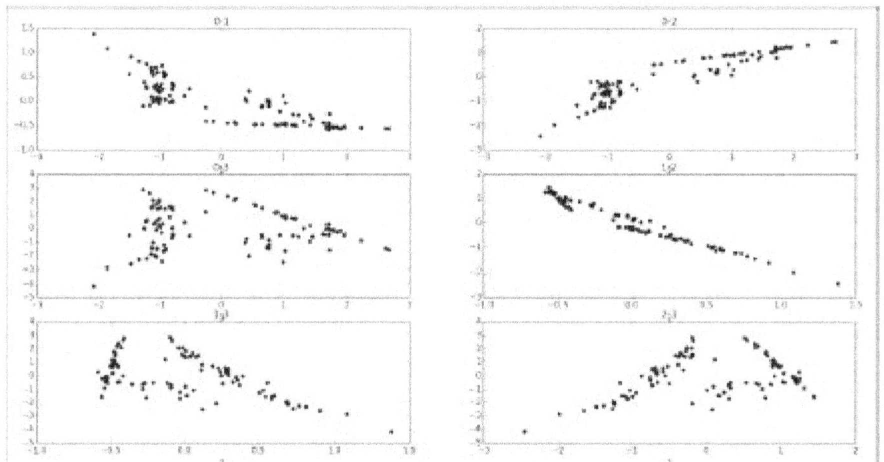

You have plotted all of the variable combinations in the figure above. The top two charts show combinations of the 0th and 1st columns, followed by the 0th and 2nd. The class designations are also used to color the points. This indicates the amount of information available for variable combinations needed to conduct a classification job.

How to Achieve It

You need to do two things to prepare your dataset and train your model: get a training test to get the train and test data and build your model, and train the model. Lastly, you will utilize the test model to validate the model's utility.

How it Operates

You must first get data and then plot it with plot data. It is also necessary to isolate a portion of the training data for the testing needed to decide the model. Then, to do the same thing, use the get-train test function.

You must train the test split size, which is the usual 80/20, inside the get train test function. Afterward, use 80% of the data to train your model. Now, use NumPy's column stack function to merge x and y into a single matrix before splitting.

Then, use the previously stated StratifiedShuffleSplit to achieve a consistent class label distribution across the training and test sets

You should be able to build a classifier using the following training and testing sets. The training set, class labels y, and characteristics x must be used to start the construction model. This function additionally takes, as an argument K, the number of neighbors with a default value of two. KNeighborClassifier, a scikit-learn KNN execution, is used.

Finally, to generate the model, create an object of the classifier and call its fit method.

It would help if you were prepared to test the module's performance using the training data. The training data (x and y) and model may be sent to the test model method.

You are aware of the real class labels (y). To get the expected labels, use x to activate the predict function. Print some of the model assessment metrics next. The model's accuracy, a confusion matrix, and the result of a function called the classification report can then be printed. The Scikit-metrics Learn module has a classification report function that displays several model assessment metrics.

Let's look at the model metrics:

```
Model evaluation on training set
------------------------------------------

Model accuracy - 91.25%


Confusion Matrix
==================
array([[40,  0],
       [ 7, 33]])
None

Classification Report
--------------------
             precision    recall  f1-score   support

        0.0       0.85      1.00      0.92        40
        1.0       1.00      0.82      0.90        40

avg / total       0.93      0.91      0.91        80
```

The accuracy score is 91.25 percent, as you can see. You will not repeat the definition's precision; instead, go to the introduction.

Have a look at the confusion matrix. A real positive cell is represented by the top-left cell. There should be no false negatives, but there should be seven false positives.

Finally, inside the categorization report, you have the accuracy, recall an F1 score, and support. Consider these definitions:
Precision is defined as the ratio of true positives to the total of true positives and false positives.

Accuracy is defined as the ratio of true positives to the sum of true positives and false negatives.
The harmonic mean of accuracy and sensitivity is described by an F1 score.

You will learn more about the measure mentioned above. Let's assume, for now, that we are accurate and remember things well.
It is useful to know that our model has a 91 percent accuracy, but the true test will be when it is run on test data. Consider the following metrics for the test data:

```
Model evaluation on test set
=================================

Model accuracy = 95.00%


Confusion Matrix
------------------
array([[ 9,  1],
       [ 0, 10]])
None

Classification Report
==================
              precision    recall  f1-score   support

         0.0       1.00      0.90      0.95        10
         1.0       0.91      1.00      0.95        10

avg / total       0.95      0.95      0.95        20
```

It is important to note that our model has 95 percent accuracy for the test data, which is an indication of a well-fitting model.
Let's go further into the model we've developed.
The method that gets params is called first. This method returns the values of all parameters supplied to the model. Let's go through each of the settings one by one.

The first parameter defines the KNN implementation's underlying data structure. Since each record in the training set must be compared to another record, brute force implementation may need significant resources. As a result, you may choose between kd tree and ball tree as the data structure. For each record, a brute will use the brute force approach to loop over all the documents.

Leaf size is a parameter that is sent to the kd tree or ball tree methods. Metric denotes the distance measure used to identify neighbors. The Minkowski to Euclidean distance is reduced by a p-value of two.

There is also a weight parameter. KNN chooses the test instance's class label based on the class labels of its K closest neighbors. The class label for the test instance is determined by the most votes. When the weights

are adjusted to distance, however, each neighbor is allocated a weight that is inversely proportionate to its distance. Weighted voting is used instead of a simple vote to choose the class label of a test set.
How to Classify Documents Using Naïve Bayes

For this instance, you will examine a document categorization issue. You will use the Nave Bayes classification method. The Nave Bayes algorithm is powered by the Bayes' rule.

$$P(X|Y) = \frac{P(Y|X)*P(X)}{P(Y)}$$

It shows how likely it is that event X will happen if event Y has already happened. You will now categorize the text. This is a binary classification problem: you are given a movie review and must determine if it is good or negative.

In Bayesian terminology, you must determine the conditional probability: the likelihood that the review is favorable and the likelihood that the review is negative. Here's an example:

$$P(class = positive | review), \text{and } P(class = negative | review)$$

If you know the previous two probability values for every given review, you may label it as positive or negative by comparing these numbers. If the conditional probability for a negative is greater than the conditional probability for a positive, the review may be classified as unfavorable, and vice versa.

Let's look at these probabilities using Bayes' rule:

$$P(positive|review) = \frac{P(review|positive)*P(positive)}{P(review)}$$

$$P(negative|review) = \frac{P(review|negative)*P(negative)}{P(review)}$$

You may disregard the denominator, which is a simple scaling factor, while you compare these two equations to conclude the forecast.
The posterior probability is defined as the LHS (left-hand side) of the preceding equation.

Have a look at the RHS numerator (right-hand side)

P(positive review) * P (positive)

P (positive) denotes the likelihood of a positive class. It is the expectation of favorable class label distribution based on the training set.

You will make an educated guess based on the training test. It is calculated as follows:

$$P(positive) = \frac{No\ of\ reviews\ with\ positive\ class\ label}{Total\ reviews\ in\ the\ corpus}$$

The probability is P(review|positive). It answers the question: what is the likelihood of receiving the review if the class is positive? You will again estimate it using the training set.

Before delving further into the probability equation, consider the independence assumption. Because of this assumption, the algorithm is prefixed with naive. In contrast, you think that the words appear in a paper independently of one another. This assumption will be used to determine the probability.

Have a look at the word list. Let us use the mathematical notation:

$$review = \{word_1, word_2, \ldots\ldots, word_n\}$$

Using the independence assumption, you can deduce that the likelihood of each of these terms being in a review equals the product of the individual probabilities of the component words in the study.

The likelihood equation may now be defined as follows:

$$P(review = \{word_1, word_2, \ldots, word_n\} \mid positive) = \prod_{i=1}^{n} P(word_i \mid positive)$$

Hence, given a new review, you can use the prior and likelihood formulae to determine whether the review is negative or positive.

Making decision trees to tackle issues with several classes

This section will show you how to build decision trees to handle multiclass classification problems. A decision tree is a method of arriving at an answer by asking multiple questions. A decision tree is formed by a series of if-then expressions grouped hierarchically. Due to this, it is simple to comprehend and interpret

.

In principle, a large number of decision trees may be created for a single dataset. Some trees are more precise than others. There are efficient techniques for constructing a relatively real tree in a small amount of time. Hunt's algorithm is one of these algorithms, as is CART, which is based on Hunt's algorithm.

The algorithm of the search is as follows:
Given an n-record dataset, D, with each record containing m attributes/features/columns and each record labeled y1, y2, or y3, the method proceeds as follows:

If all of the entries in D have the same class label, say y1, then y1 represents the tree's leaf node and is labeled as y1.
A feature test condition is used to split the records into smaller subsets if D includes a form that belongs to more than one class label.

For example, suppose you execute a feature test condition on all the characteristics during the first run and uncover a single property that may divide the datasets into three smaller groups. The property is elevated to the position of the root node. To find the next level of nodes, we apply the test condition to all three subgroups. This procedure is repeated iteratively.

Recall that after your classification is defined, you must specify three class labels, y1, y2, and y3. This is an issue with several classes. The Iris dataset, which has been utilized in the majority of the examples, is a three-class issue. The records are divided into three categories. This can be generalized into an n-class issue. Digit recognition is an excellent example in which you must classify a specific picture in one of the digits ranging from zero to nine. The majority of real-world situations are essentially multiclass. Some algorithms can also handle scenarios with several classes. These algorithms do not need any changes. The method mentioned in the following chapters can address multiclass problems.

Multiclass issues may be handled via Nave Bayes, KNN algorithms, and Decision trees. Let's look at how decision trees may be used to solve multiclass situations. It is also advantageous to be well-versed in decision trees.

Let's get started with our decision tree:
To explain how to design decision trees, we will use the Iris dataset. Decision trees are non-parametric supervised learning approaches for solving classification and regression issues. As previously stated, there are several advantages to employing decision trees.
Some of the benefits are as follows:

These are simple to understand.
They need little data preparation and feature conversion.
They are inherently supportive of multiclass issues.

Decision trees are not without flaws. Some of the issues they create are as follows:

There may be more than a million trees that match a given dataset.
They are prone to overfitting. Accuracy in a training set is high, but performance with test data is low.

The class imbalance issue may have a significant influence on decision trees. In a binary classification issue, the class imbalance problem occurs when the training set does not include an equal number of cases for both class labels. This also applies to multiclass problems.

The property test condition is the most significant component of decision trees. Let's look at the following feature test condition. In general, any instance attribute may be understood or not.

A **binary attribute** is one in which a property may have two alternative values, such as true or false. In the following example, the property test condition should return two values.

Nominal attribute: A property that may take more than two values, for example, n values. The property test condition should either show output n or divide it into binary splits.

Ordinal attribute: This is when there is an implied order in their values. Consider a hypothetical characteristic named size, which may take the values small, medium, or massive. The attribute may have three values, which are listed in the following order: small, medium, and big. They are addressed by the feature property test condition, which is analogous to the nominal attribute.

Continuous characteristics are those that can take continuous values. They are then classified as ordinal characteristics and handled.

A property test condition is a method of dividing input records into subsets based on the criterion or measure known as impunity. This impunity is calculated for each attribute in the instance using the class label. The characteristic that contributes the most immunity is chosen as the data splitting attribute, or in other words, the node for that level in the tree.

Let's look at an example to better understand it. To calculate impunity, you will use a metric called entropy.
The following is a definition of entropy:

$$E(X) = -\sum_{i=1}^{n} P(x_i) \log_2 \left(P(x_i) \right)$$

Imagine the following scenario:

X= {2,2}

With the aforementioned technique, you can now calculate the entropy given the following values.

With this formula, the entropy result is 0. A value of 0 denotes homogeneity. Entropy is simple to program in Python.

You will use entropy to get the best splitting variable possible. Then, using the following formula, calculate the entropy based on the class labels:

$$Entropy(t) = -\sum_{i=0}^{c-1} p(i|t)\log_2 p(i|t)$$

Let us now define a new word called information gain. This is a metric for determining which property in a given instance is helpful in distinguishing different class labels.

The difference between the entropy of the parent and the average entropy of the offspring nodes is referred to as information gain. You will use the information obtained to construct the tree at each stage.

To begin, calculate the general entropy for all characteristics in a training set. Imagine the following scenario:

Lead Actor	Oscar Winning	Box Office	Watch
Y	Y	N	Y
Y	N	Y	N
N	N	Y	Y
N	Y	Y	Y

The preceding dataset shows fictitious data acquired for a user to determine the kind of movies he or she is interested in. There are four features: the first is whether the user watches a movie based on the leading actor, the second is whether the user chooses to watch the film based on whether or not it won an Oscar, and the third is whether the user decides to watch a movie based on its box office performance.

To build a decision tree for the above example, first, compute the entropy of the whole dataset. Since this is a two-class issue, c=2. Moreover, there are four records, and the entropy of the complete dataset is as follows:

$$E(D) = -\left(\frac{1}{4} * \log_2\left(\frac{1}{4}\right) + \frac{3}{4} * \log_2\left(\frac{3}{4}\right) \right)$$

The dataset has a general entropy of 0.811.

Let us now look at the first attribute, the lead attribute. There is a single class label that reads Y and another that says N for the principal actor, Y. Both the instance class labels for the leading actor, N, are N.

As demonstrated, you will calculate the average entropy:

```
entropy_lead_actor_Y = 2/4.0 * -(1/2.0 * log(1/2.0,2) + 1/2.0 * log(1/2.0 ,2))
entropy_lead_actor_N = 2/4.0 * -(0   + 2/2.0 * log(2/2.0,2))
entroyp_lead_actor - entropy_lead_actor_Y + entropy_lead_actor_N
```

There are two records with Y as the main actor and two records with N as the lead actor. As a result, the entropy value is multiplied by 2/4.

Once the entropy for this specific subset of data is generated, you will note that one of the two records has a class label of Y, while the other has a class label of N for the lead actor Y. In addition, both albums carry the class label N for the starring actor N. As a result, we calculate the average entropy for this specific property.

The main actor attribute has an average entropy value of 0.5.

The knowledge gain is 0.311 (0.811-0.5).

You will also compute the information gained for each characteristic. The qualities with the most information earn the win and become the decision tree's root node.

The same procedure is used to calculate the nodes' second level, and so on.

How it Operates

Let's start with the most important function. To begin, you will use get data in the variables x, y, and label names to obtain the Iris dataset. You take the label names so that when you see the correctness of your model, you may quantify it by individual labels. The Iris data, as previously stated, has a three-class difficulty. It would help if you created a classifier that can classify any new instances into one of the three kinds.

Next, use the build model function to generate a decision tree on the training data. The DecisionTreeClassifier class constructs a decision tree using the scikit-learn model tree.

The model is a tree.
DecisionTreeClassifier(criterion="entropy")
The feature test condition is given, as you can see. The model may then be created by executing the fit function and returned to the caller application.

Let us now use the test model function to calculate the model. The model takes instances x and class labels y, as well as the decision tree model and the class label names.
Scikit-module learns metric has three assessment criteria.

```
from sklearn.metrics import
accuracy_score,classification_report,confusion_matrix
```

We defined accuracy in earlier sections.

The confusion matrix described in the first part is output by a confusion matrix. A confusion matrix is a helpful tool for calculating model performance. The cell values with genuine positive and false positive values are of particular interest to us.

Finally, the classification report shows the recall, precision, and F1 score. Then, we must calculate the model on the training data.

```
Model accuracy = 100.00%


Confusion Matrix
------------------
array([[40,  0,  0],
       [ 0, 40,  0],
       [ 0,  0, 40]])
None
[[40  0  0]
 [ 0 40  0]
 [ 0  0  0]]

Classification Report
=================
              precision    recall  f1-score   support

      setosa       1.00      1.00      1.00        40
  versicolor       1.00      1.00      1.00        40
   virginica       1.00      1.00      1.00        40

 avg / total       1.00      1.00      1.00       120
```

You have now done an outstanding job with the training dataset. You have a 100% accuracy rate. The real test is when the rubber meets the road, with the test dataset.

Chapter 9:

Predictions using Linear Regression

The most often utilized statistical approach is Linear regression analysis. It is the investigation of linear, additive relationships between variables. It is often utilized in industries to create models that will help a firm. For example, in the retail business, there are several elements that influence the selling of a product. Some of these characteristics might be promotions, pricing, or seasonality. A linear regression model enables one to analyze the impact of each of these variables on product sales as well as calculate the baseline sales, which indicate the number of sales of this product in the absence of external influences such as promotions, and so on.

Simple Linear Regression
A basic linear regression has one variable and is stated in the following format:

Y = A + Bx

The dependent variable is y, the independent variable is x, the intercept is A, and the co-efficient is B.

The dataset you'll be using will include a sample of men's height (cm) and weight (kg).

This code reads the data and makes a simple scatter plot to show how weight and height are distributed:

```
>>> import numpy as np
>>> import pandas as pd
>>> from scipy import stats
>>> import matplotlib.pyplot as plt
>>> sl_data = pd.read_csv('Data/Mens_height_weight.csv')
>>> fig, ax = plt.subplots(1, 1)
>>> ax.scatter(sl_data['Height'],sl_data['Weight'])
>>> ax.set_xlabel('Height')
>>> ax.set_ylabel('Weight')
>>> plt.show()
```

The following is the output of the aforementioned code:

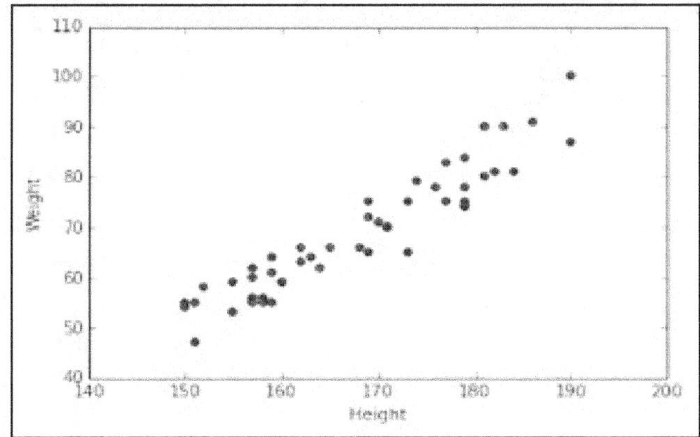

The graphic shows that there is a linear link between the individual's weight and height.

Let's look at how the variables are connected to one another:
```
>>>sl_data.corr()
```

The following correlation matrix is shown by the code above:

	Height	Weight
Height	1.000000	0.942603
Weight	0.942603	1.000000

The Pearson correlation value coefficient of 0.94 clearly shows that height and weight are associated with each other. A Pearson correlation goes from -1 to + 1; thus, when the value is higher, the relationship between the two variables is more significant, whether they rise or fall together. If the correlation value is negative, the relationship between the two variables is strong but skewed.

Create a linear regression model using weight as the dependent variable and x as the independent variable.

```
>>># Create linear regression object
>>> lm = linear_model.LinearRegression()
>>># Train the model using the training sets
>>> lm.fit(sl_data.Height[:,np.newaxis], sl_data.Weight)
>>> print 'Intercept is ' + str(lm.intercept_) + '\n'
Intercept is -99.2772096063
>>> print 'Coefficient value of the height is ' + str(lm.coef_) + '\n'
Coefficient value of the height is [ 1.00092142]
>>> print pd.DataFrame(zip(sl_data.columns,lm.coef_),
columns = ['features', 'estimatedCoefficients'])
```

The above code produces the following result:

	features	estimatedCoefficients
0	Height	1.000921

The linear model is used in the preceding code. To create a linear regression object, use the linear regression (). The fit () approach of 1m is then used to define the dependent and independent variables; in this example, the weight is the dependent variable, and the height is the independent variable.

To get the intercept value, use 1m.intercept_, and to obtain the coefficient, use 1m.coef.

The last line of code aids in the construction of a DataFrame of the independent variable and its accompanying coefficients. This will be important when you investigate multiple regression in depth.

Next, using the trend line, plot the scatter chart to achieve the following result:

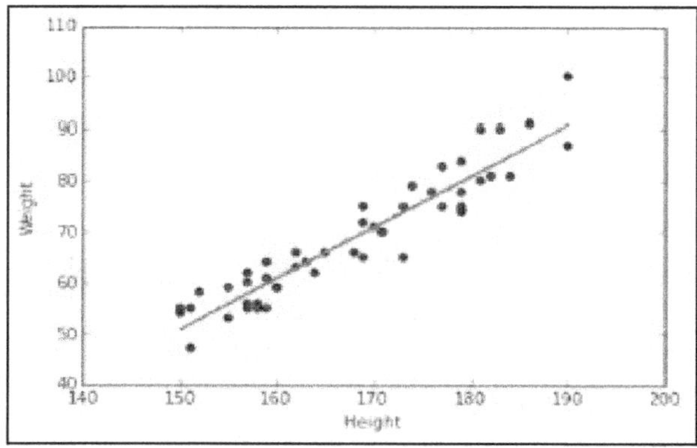

Multiple Regression

When more than one independent variable is used to anticipate a dependent variable, multiple linear regression occurs.

$$Y' = a + b_1 x_1 + b_2 x_2 + \ldots\ldots + b_n x_n$$

In the formula above, y represents the dependent variable, a represents the intercept, b1, and b2 represent the coefficients, and x1 and x2 represent the independent variables.

To develop the multiple linear regression model, you'll need to utilize NBA basketball data to anticipate average points per game.

The data column descriptions are as follows:

Height: Indicates height in feet.
Weight: The weight expressed in pounds.
Success field goals. The percentage of successful field goals.
Success free throws. The percentage of successful free throws.
Avg points scored. The average number of points scored each game.

The code below loads the aforementioned data, and then you use the DataFrame's describe () function to get the univariate metrics for each field.

```
>>> b_data = pd.read_csv('Data/basketball.csv')
>>> b_data.describe()
```

The following is the output of the preceding code:

	height	weight	success_field_goals	success_free_throws	avg_points_scored
count	54.000000	54.000000	54.000000	54.000000	54.000000
mean	6.587037	209.907407	0.449111	0.741852	11.790741
std	0.458894	30.265036	0.056551	0.100146	5.890257
min	5.700000	105.000000	0.291000	0.244000	2.800000
25%	6.225000	185.000000	0.415250	0.713000	8.150000
50%	6.650000	212.500000	0.443500	0.753500	10.750000
75%	6.900000	235.000000	0.483500	0.795250	13.600000
max	7.600000	263.000000	0.599000	0.900000	27.400000

The following observations may be drawn from the data table above:

A basketball player's average height is close to 6.5 feet.

The player with the smallest stature is 5.7 feet.

The tallest player is 7.7 feet tall.

The minimal weight for the player is 105 pounds.

The player with the most weight is 263 pounds.

A player's most significant field goal percentage is about 60%.

A player's lowest field goal percentage is roughly 29%.

The average field goal rate for a player is 45%; however, based on the modest standard deviation, most players have a field goal rate of 40% to 50%.

Among the free shots, one player skips 3/4 of the game.

The top free throw shooter has a success percentage of 90%.

The majority of the players have a free throw success percentage of 70-80%.

A player's highest score per game is roughly 27.

The least possible score is 3

The players average 12 points each game.

Let's look at the relationship between the variables:

```
>>>b_data.corr()
```

This is the output of the preceding code:

	height	weight	success_field_goals	success_free_throws	avg_points_scored
height	1.000000	0.834324	0.495546	-0.259271	-0.068906
weight	0.834324	1.000000	0.518051	-0.290159	-0.009844
success_field_goals	0.495546	0.516051	1.000000	-0.018570	0.338760
success_free_throws	-0.259271	-0.290150	-0.018570	1.000000	0.244852
avg_points_scored	-0.068906	-0.009844	0.338760	0.244852	1.000000

The following may be deduced from the above table:
Height and weight have a strong relationship.
A slight positive association exists between successful field goals and weight and height.
The mean points achieved have the most link with success field goals, although they aren't very strong.

Now consider the distribution of each of the independent variables in relation to the dependent variable:
The result is as follows:

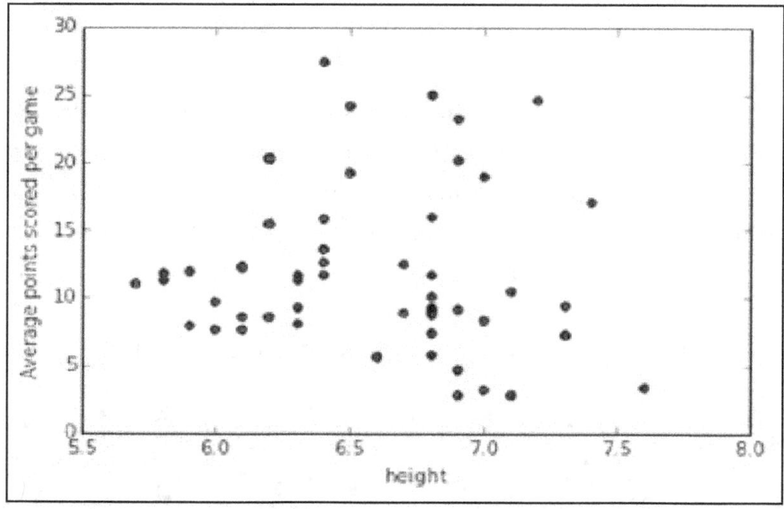

The scatter plot below shows that there is no real relationship between the average points achieved and the height. The distribution looks to be rather erratic.

Let's look at the relationship between average points scored and weight:

```
>>> fig, ax = plt.subplots(1, 1)
>>> ax.scatter(b_data.weight, b_data.avg_points_scored)
>>> ax.set_xlabel('weight')
>>> ax.set_ylabel('Average points scored per game')
>>> plt.show()
```

This is the result:

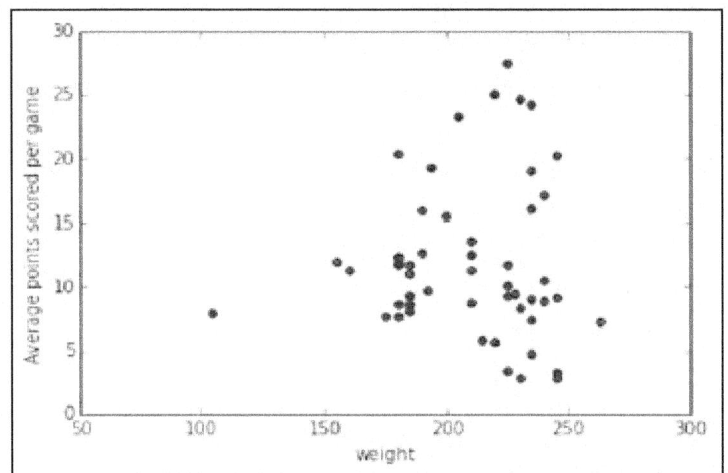

You'll see that 105 pounds are an exception, with a considerably lower average point score. You can also see that the players that weighed close to 240 pounds had the most range in the score. As a result, the theory may be made taller and heavier, with a higher score. The shorter and heavier players, on the other hand, have a minimal score.

Let us now investigate the relationship between successful field goals and average points attained:

```
>>> fig, ax = plt.subplots(1, 1)
>>> ax.scatter(b_data.success_field_goals, b_data.avg_points_scored)
>>> ax.set_xlabel('success_field_goals')
>>> ax.set_ylabel('Average points scored per game')
>>> plt.show()
```

The previous code's output is shown below:

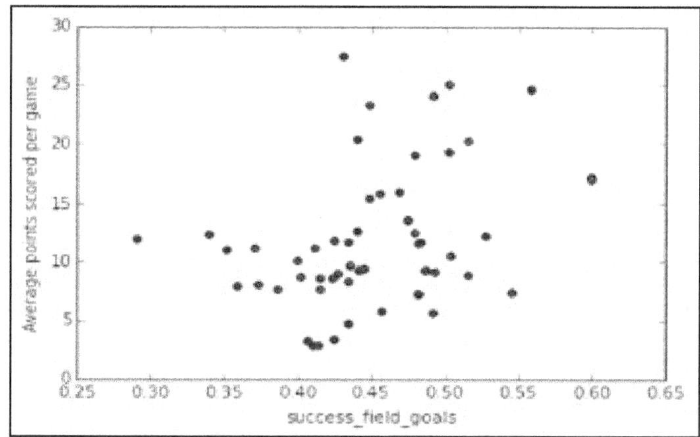

The success field _goals variable has a linear connection with the average number of points earned, but the distribution is skewed.

Next, consider the relationship between successful free throws and average points scored per game:

```python
>>> fig, ax = plt.subplots(1, 1)
>>> ax.scatter(b_data.success_free_throws, b_data.avg_points_scored)
>>> x.set_xlabel('success_free_throws')
>>> ax.set_ylabel('Average points scored per game')
>>> plt.show()
```

The output of the above code is as follows:

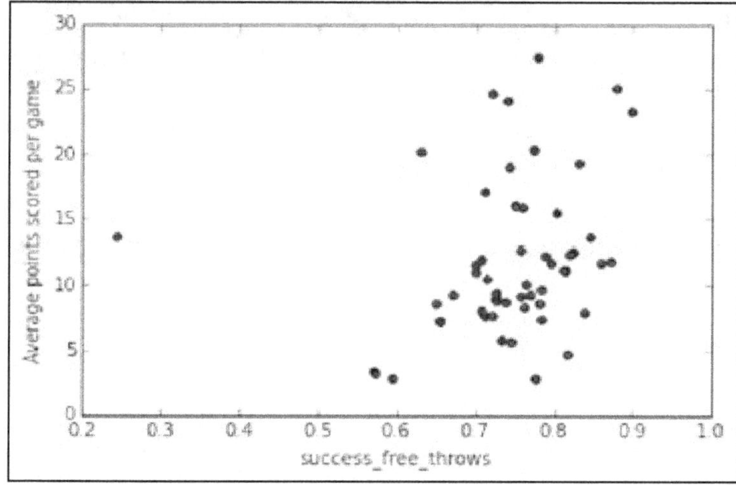

You can see that one player's free throws aren't very excellent, yet his average points per game look to be near average when compared to other players. This indicates that he would be better at half-field goals or would try more times to score. The overall distribution is also a little erratic.

According to the previous correlation and distribution analyzers, there are no evident connections between the average points obtained and the independent variables. It is reasonable to predict that the model developed using current data will be inaccurate.

Training and Testing a Model
In this part, you will split data into training and test sets:

```
>>> from sklearn import linear_model,cross_validation,
feature_selection,preprocessing
>>> import statsmodels.formula.api as sm
>>> from statsmodels.tools.eval_measures import mse
>>> from statsmodels.tools.tools import add_constant
>>> from sklearn.metrics import mean_squared_error
>>> X = b_data.values.copy()
>>> X_train, X_valid, y_train, y_valid =
cross_validation.train_test_split( X[:, :-1],
X[:, -1],
train_size=0.80)
```

Then, use values to convert the into an array structure. b data is copied (). Next, for 80% of the data, use SciKit's train test split cross validation method to divide it into training and test sets..

You will learn how to design linear regression models using the following packages:

Statsmodels is a module.
SciKit is a software program.

However, pandas include an Ordinary Least Squares (OLS) regression, which you may try after finishing this chapter. The ordinary least squares approach is used to find unknown coefficients and intercepts in a regression equation. We'll begin with the statsmodels package. The statsmodels Python module defines a tool that allows users to examine data, approximate statistical models, and run statistical tests. For each data type and estimator, a full array of descriptive statistics, charting tools, and outcome statistics is provided.

The OLS function aids in the construction of a linear regression object with a dependent and independent variable. The fit () technique may be used to fit the model. Remember that the added constant() method is used to calculate the intercept when developing the model. The OLS () function does not calculate the intercept by default, and it must be explicitly stated with the help of the add constant function. The screenshot below is a summary of the trained regression model. The following metrics are shown in the screenshot:

OLS Regression Results

Dep. Variable:	y	R-squared:	0.205
Model:	OLS	Adj. R-squared:	0.187
Method:	Least Squares	F-statistic:	3.423
Date:	Sun, 22 Mar 2015	Prob (F-statistic):	0.0174
Time:	05:11:41	Log-Likelihood:	-130.25
No. Observations:	43	AIC:	270.5
Df Residuals:	38	BIC:	279.3
Df Model:	4		
Covariance Type:	nonrobust		

	coef	std err	t	P>|t|	[95.0% Conf. Int.]
const	15.5129	16.147	0.961	0.343	-17.175 48.200
x1	-5.9277	3.066	-1.933	0.061	-12.135 0.279
x2	0.0162	0.049	0.332	0.742	-0.082 0.115
x3	55.1647	19.044	2.897	0.006	16.612 93.717

Omnibus:	6.717	Durbin-Watson:	1.637
Prob(Omnibus):	0.035	Jarque-Bera (JB):	5.457
Skew:	0.786	Prob(JB):	0.0653
Kurtosis:	3.759	Cond. No.	5.20e+03

The model is described in detail in the synopsis above. The r fair value is the most important parameter to examine; this value indicates how much of the variance of the dependent variable is captured by the model. The p-value may vary from 0 to 1, and it reflects if the model is meaningful.

The preceding output shows that the R-square value is 0.265, which is not in the field. As you can see, the model considers x3 to be the most important variable, which is the success field goals variable. In general, any p-value less than 0.05 for a variable may be deemed significant.
Now, let's create the model using the successful field goals variable and see how it does.

OLS Regression Results

Dep. Variable:	y	R-squared:	0.078
Model:	OLS	Adj. R-squared:	0.056
Method:	Least Squares	F-statistic:	3.492
Date:	Sun, 22 Mar 2015	Prob (F-statistic):	0.0688
Time:	05:11:44	Log-Likelihood:	-135.11
No. Observations:	43	AIC:	274.2
Df Residuals:	41	BIC:	277.7
Df Model:	1		
Covariance Type:	nonrobust		

	coef	std err	t	P>|t|	[95.0% Conf. Int.]
const	-2.5735	7.546	-0.341	0.735	-17.814 12.667
x1	31.4348	16.823	1.869	0.069	-2.539 65.409

Omnibus:	5.440	Durbin-Watson:	1.810
Prob(Omnibus):	0.066	Jarque-Bera (JB):	4.382
Skew:	0.760	Prob(JB):	0.112
Kurtosis:	3.370	Cond. No.	23.1

The variable has become less essential, and the r square value has decreased. The preceding model may be performed many times with various variable sets until the optimal model is discovered.
Apply both models to the test data and calculate the average squared error between the actual and projected values. The ideal model is the one with the smallest mean squared error.

```
>>>ypred = result.predict(add_constant(X_valid))
>>> print mse(ypred,y_valid)
```

To predict the specific test dataset, you add the prediction function of the regression model object in this code.

```
>>> ypred_alternate = result_alternate.predict(add_constant(X_valid[:,
2]))
>>> print mse(ypred_alternate,y_valid)
26.3
```

You'll see that the second model has a smaller mean squared error than the first.

Now, using the following code, draw the projected vs. actual plot for both models:

```
>>> fig, ax = plt.subplots(1, 1)
>>> ax.scatter(y_valid, ypred)
>>> ax.set_xlabel('Actual')
>>> ax.set_ylabel('Predicted')
>>> plt.show(
```

The outcome of the preceding code is shown below:

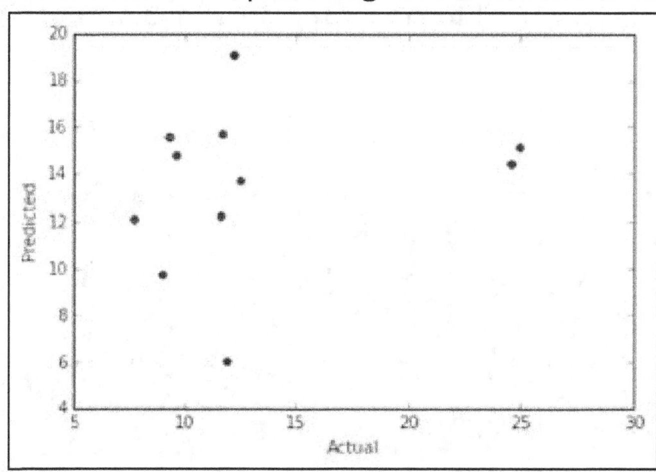

Let us now plot the scatter for the alternative model:

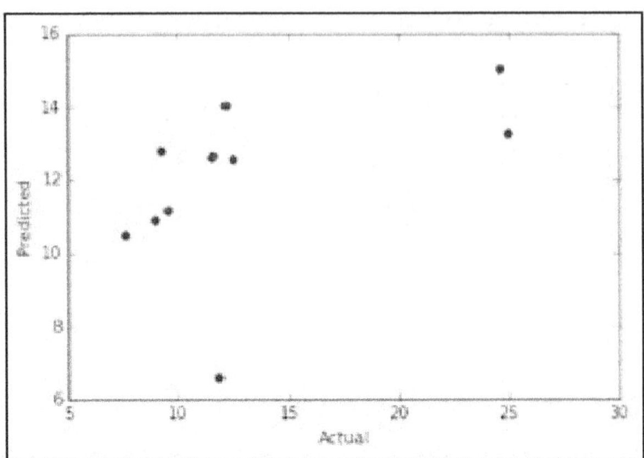

This clearly demonstrates that the models are inadequate since the predictions are not completely random.

Other factors that have an influence on the average points earned are required to develop an appropriate model.

The statsmodels package was used to create the prior model. You will next use SciKit to create a model.

This code creates a Linear Regression object, which is subsequently filled with dependent and independent variables:

```
# Create linear regression object
>>> lm = linear_model.LinearRegression()
# Train the model using the training sets
>>> lm.fit(X_train, y_train)
>>> print 'Intercept is %f' % lm.intercept_)
Intercept is 15.5129271596
>>> pd.DataFrame(zip(b_data.columns,lm.coef_), columns = ['features',
'estimatedCoefficients'])
```

The following is the output of the preceding code:

	features	estimatedCoefficients
0	height	-5.927749
1	weight	0.016150
2	success_field_goals	55.164717
3	success_free_throws	9.725042

The coefficients and intercepts are comparable to the model produced using the statsmodel program.

The SciKit package's cross-validation module is used to calculate the r square SciKit.

```
>>> cross_validation.cross_val_score(lm, X_train,
y_train, scoring='r2')
array([-0.3043391 , -0.42402161, 0.26890649])
```

Many rounds of cross-validation occur, and by default, it is 3, resulting in three results in the preceding output.

The highest value is significant, and you can see that it is identical to the one you made with statsmodels.

Let's look at how to calculate the mean squared error:

```
>>> ypred = lm.predict(X_valid)
>>> mean_squared_error(ypred,y_valid)
35.208
```

It would help if you used the SciKit package's mean squared error function:

Finally, the actual versus projected plot will be comparable to statsmodels' first model plot:

```
>>> fig, ax = plt.subplots(1, 1)
>>> ax.scatter(y_valid, ypred)
>>> ax.set_xlabel('Actual')
>>> ax.set_ylabel('Predicted')
>>> plt.show()
```

The result is as follows:

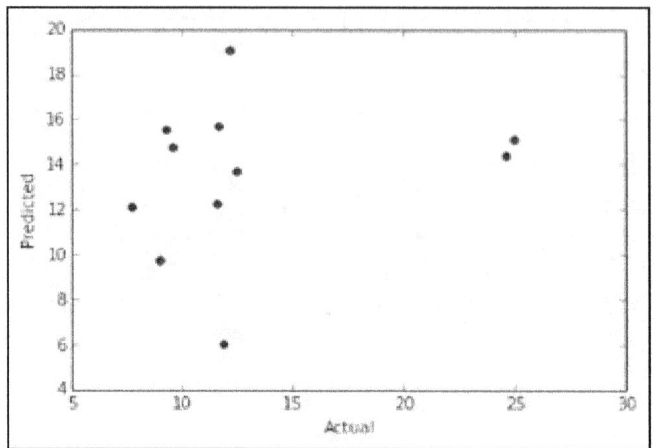

This chapter concentrated on creating a basic regression model as well as numerous regressions. When the data was subjected to a first inspection study in order to comprehend it. The regression model was then created using statsmodels and the SciKit package.

Chapter 10:

Data Analysis-Deep dive

Dimensionality reduction will be the emphasis of this Chapter. High-dimensional data is ubiquitous in today's world. Consider creating a product suggestion engine for a small e-commerce website. Even with different items, there are several factors to consider. Another area with high-dimensional data is bioinformatics. Microarray datasets with hundreds of dimensions are used to analyze gene expression.

If your purpose is to either examine the data or prepare it for use by an algorithm, excessive dimensionality, sometimes known as the curse of dimensionality, is a big impediment. To cope with this, you need effective solutions. Also, the number of dimensions makes most existing data mining methods even more difficult to use. As the number of dimensions goes up, the techniques become impossible to compute, making them useless for most applications.

13

intact as feasible while reducing the number of dimensions. As a result, since we have a reduced dimension in the confined feature space, the implementation time of the algorithms is constrained. Since the structure of the data is kept, the results may be the closest thing to the original data space. Keeping the structure means two things: first, that the differences in the original dataset don't change, and second, that the distance between the data and vectors in the new projected space stays the same.

Decomposition of a Matrix

Matrix decomposition produces many dimensionality reduction strategies. The data is often arranged as a matrix, with instances in rows and characteristics in columns. A matrix decomposition technique is a method of representing a matrix. Assume A is a product of two additional matrices, B and C. The matrix B is designed to include vectors that may explain the data change. The magnitude of this fluctuation is expected to be stored in matrix C. As a result, the original matrix A is now represented as a linear combination of B and C.

The techniques you'll see in the next sections use matrices to accomplish dimensionality reduction. Some methods, like principal component analysis, stress that the real vectors must be perpendicular to each other. Other methods, like dictionary learning, don't do this.

In the next chapter, we'll see some of these strategies in action:
Mining the Principal Components

The Principal Component Analysis is the first approach you will examine (PCA). PCA is a kind of unsupervised approach. In multivariate situations, PCA is used to reduce the dimension of the data with the least amount of information loss. In other words, keeping the data as varied as possible. It denotes the direction in which the data is scattered to the greatest extent.

Imagine the following scenario:

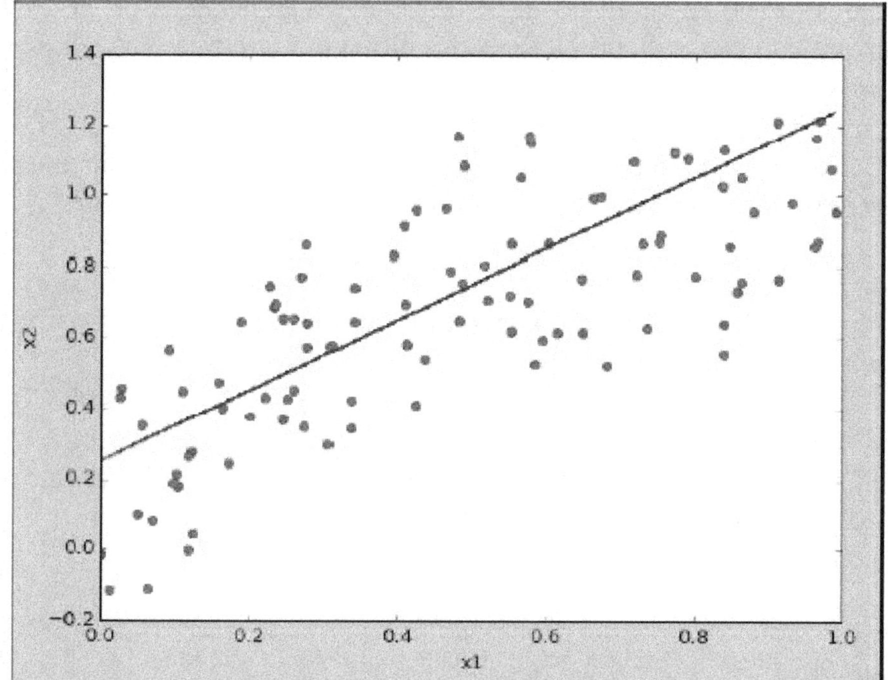

You've got a scatter plot with two variables, x1 and x2. The diagonal line has the most variety. The goal of using PCA is to keep the variation's direction. Instead of utilizing the direction of two variables, x1, and x2, to describe this data, the goal is to find a vector represented by the blue line and designate the data only using this vector. In general, you wish to reduce the data dimension from two to one.

This blue line vector will be determined using the mathematical tools Eigenvalues and Eigenvectors. Recall that variance represents the degree of dispersion in the data. But when there is only one dimension, it is easy to show a correlation between variables as a matrix. By using the standard deviation to make the values of the covariance matrix equal, you can make a correlation matrix. The covariance matrix represents a 2 x 2 matrix containing two variables, x1, and x2, and it determines how these two variables move in the same direction in the following scenario.

When you do an Eigenvalue decomposition or get the Eigenvectors and Eigenvalues of the covariance matrix, the major Eigenvector, or largest Eigenvalue, is in the direction where the preliminary data has the most variation.

In our scenario, this ought to be the vector that the blue line on the graph represents. The data that was given will then be put on this blue line vector to get the smaller dimension.

PCA may be performed on both the covariance and correlation matrices. Remember that if you use a dataset with different scales in the PCA, the result may not be useful.

The Iris dataset will next be used to demonstrate how to effectively utilize PCA in molding the dataset's dimension. The Iris dataset contains data on 150 iris blossoms from three distinct species.
The Iris dataset is divided into three classes:

Iris Setosa
Versicolor Iris
Virginia Iris

The following are four Iris dataset properties:

The length of the sepals in centimeters
The petal width in centimeters
The petal length in centimeters
The breadth of the sepals in centimeters

Our goal is to minimize the data's dimension. In the following example, we have four columns of instances. Let's say you're making a classifier to figure out what kind of flower a new image shows. Can you do this assignment using instances from the reduced dimension space? Is it possible to cut the number of columns in our classifier from four to two while keeping a high level of accuracy?
PCA is accomplished by doing the following steps:

Standardize the dataset such that the mean value is zero.

Determine the correlation matrix and unit standard deviation value for the dataset.

Separate the Eigenvectors and values of the correlation matrix.

In decreasing order, choose the best eigenvectors based on the Eigenvalues.

In the new subspace, translate the input Eigenvectors matrix.

Now, you will normalize this data by giving it a mean of 0 and a standard deviation of 1, and then use the numpyscorrcoef function to find the correlation matrix:

```
x_s = scale(x,with_mean=True,with_std=True,axis=0)
x_c = np.corrcoef(x_s.T)
```

After that, you should decompose the Eigenvalues and project the Iris data onto the top two primary Eigenvectors. Finally, you will visualize the dataset in the tight space. The code to use is as follows:

```
eig_val,r_eig_vec = scipy.linalg.eig(x_c)
print 'Eigen values \n%s'%(eig_val)
print '\n Eigen vectors \n%s'%(r_eig_vec)
# Select the first two eigen vectors.
w = r_eig_vec[:,0:2]
# # Project the dataset in to the
dimension
# from 4 dimension to 2 using the right
eignen vector
x_rd = x_s.dot(w)
# Scatter plot the new two dimensions
plt.figure(1)
plt.scatter(x_rd[:,0],x_rd[:,1],c=y)
plt.xlabel("Component 1")
plt.ylabel("Component 2")
```

Scaling, centering, and standardizing may all be accomplished with the scale function. Subtraction of the mean value from different values is referred to as centering. Scaling is the process of dividing each value by the standard deviation of the variable, while standardization is the process of centering followed by scaling. The scale may be used to do all three normalizing procedures by using variables with the _mean and _std functions.

How it Operates

There are four columns in the Iris dataset. Even if there aren't many columns, it serves its job. The goal is to decrease the dimensionality of the Iris dataset to two from four while keeping storing all of the data's features.

You'll use scikit-load iris learn's method to load the Iris data into the x and y variables. The x variables constitute a data matrix, and its form is as follows:

>>>x.shape.

(150, 4)

>>>

The data matrix x will be scaled to have a zero mean and a unit standard deviation. The general guideline is that if all of the columns in your data are measured using the same scale and have the same unit of measurement, you don't need to scale the data. This will allow PCA to capture these fundamental units with the greatest variance.

You may now generate a correlation matrix using our provided data.
The correlation matrix X1... Xn containing n random variables is, therefore, x n matrix whosei, jentry is corr (Xi, Xj).

The Eigenvalues and Eigenvectors of the matrix will then be computed using the SciPy module. Please have a look at our Eigenvalues and Eigenvectors.

```
print Eigen values \n%s%(eig_val)
print \n Eigen vectors \n%s%(r_eig_vec)
```

The result is as follows:

```
Eigen values
[ 2.91081808+0.j  0.92122093+0.j  0.14735328+0.j  0.02060771+0.j]

 Eigen vectors
[[ 0.52237162 -0.37231836 -0.72101681  0.26199559]
 [-0.26335492 -0.92555649  0.24203288 -0.12413481]
 [ 0.58125401 -0.02109478  0.14089226 -0.80115427]
 [ 0.56561105 -0.06541577  0.6338014   0.52354627]]
```

In the above example, the Eigenvalues are shown in decreasing order. The most pressing issue is the quantity of components from which to choose. The next part will teach you how to calculate the number of components in several methods.

You'll see that you only choose the first two columns of the right-hand side Eigenvectors. The discriminating capacity of the retained components on the Y variable is an excellent test of how variance in the data is kept.

Next, plot the components along the x and y axes and color them with the target variable.

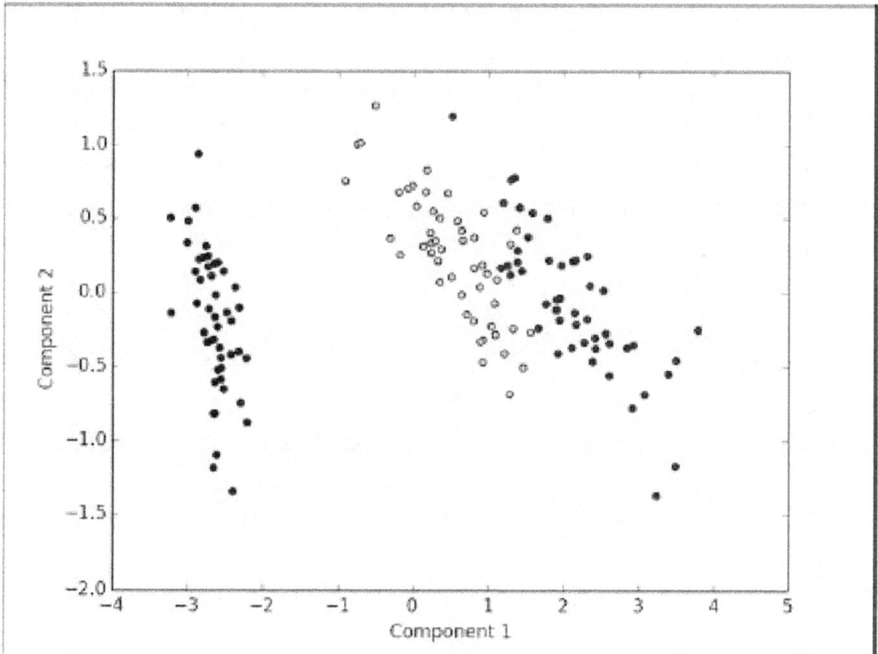

It is worth noting that components 1 and 2 may distinguish between the three types of iris blooms. So, you can use PCA to reduce the number of dimensions from four to two while still being able to tell which iris flower examples belong to which class.

Here are some other methods for determining the amount of components required. Following is a list of empirical approaches for selecting the components:

1. The Eigenvalue criterion.
An Eigenvalue of one indicates that the component would describe the variability of the variable.
2. The percentage of the variance explained criterion.

You print the Eigenvalue, the percentage of the total variation that each component represents, and the total percentage of the total variation for each component. For example, component 1 has an Eigenvalue of 2.91, and 2.91/4 represents the percentage of variance, which is 72.80%. If you combine the first two components, you can explain 95.80% of the variation in the data.

A correlation matrix's decomposition into Eigenvectors and values is a generic approach that may be applied to any matrix. In the next example, you will utilize it in a correlation matrix to understand the primary axes of the data distribution, i.e., the axes across which the greatest variance in the data is seen.

PCA can be used to find out more about a problem or to prepare data for another algorithm. Document classification dataset difficulties are often associated with advanced dimensional feature vectors. Before sending the data to a classification system, PCA can be used to reduce the number of dimensions in the dataset to just the most important ones.

The main downside of PCA is that it is computationally costly. Finally, the corrcoeff function will internally normalize your data as part of its calculation.

Using the Kernel PCA

PCA makes the assumption that all of the major directions of variation in the data are straight lines. This is not the case in the majority of real-world datasets.

In this example, we will look at the kernel PCA, which will allow us to minimize the dimension of the dataset when the variance is not straight lines.

The kernel function is employed in all data points in Kernel PCA. The input data is now in kernel space. A typical PCA is carried out in kernel space.

The iris dataset will not be used in the next step; instead, you will generate a dataset with modifications that are not straight lines. You will not be able to do a basic PCA on this dataset in this manner.

How it Operates

The first step is to create a dataset using scikit's data creation function. In this example, you will utilize the make circles function. We can make two concentric circles, one bigger and one smaller. Each concentric circle represents a distinct class. As a result, you construct a two-class issue using two concentric circles.

Now, let's look at the data that was created. The make circles method creates a 400-by-400-pixel dataset with two dimensions. The following are plots of the primary data:

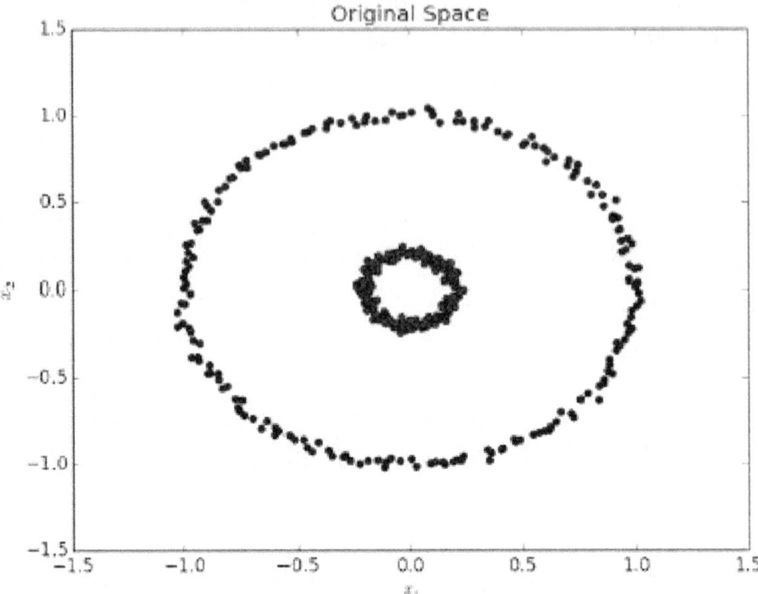

The graph above shows how the data has been distributed. The outside circle is from class one, while the inner circle is from class two. Is it feasible to use this data to train a linear classifier? You will not be able to do this. The data changes are not in a straight line. As a result, standard PCA cannot be used. To alter the data, you will use the kernel PCA.

Before we go into kernel PCA, let's see what occurs with a standard PCA on this dataset.

Let's have a look at the output plots for the first two components:
According to the preceding figure, the PCA members are unable to discern between the two classes in a linear method.

Let's see how the first component's class separates ability.
This graph, of which you only showed the first part, shows that PCA can't separate the data.

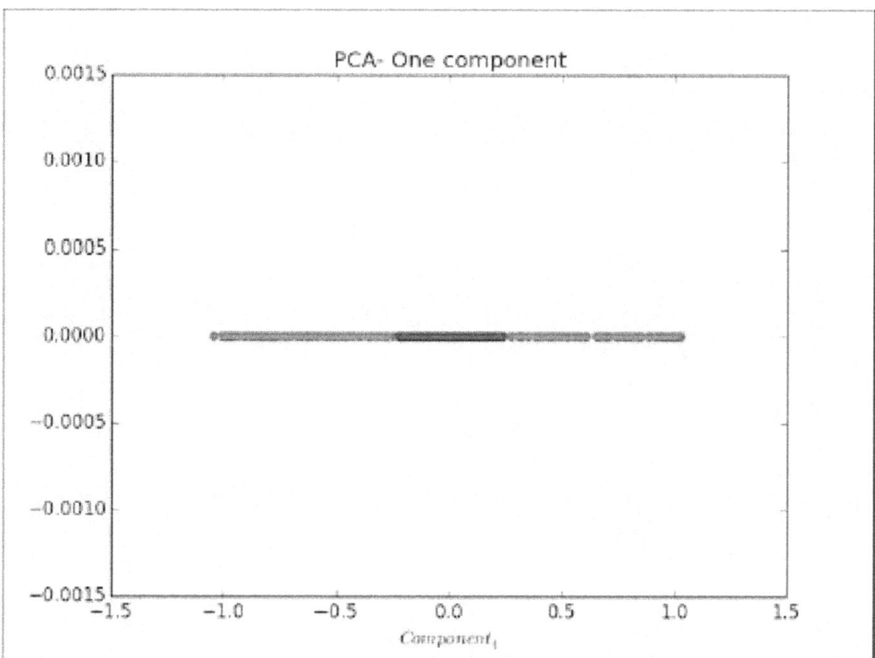

The most common PCA method is a linear projection approach that works well if the data can be separated linearly. When the data can't be separated in a linear way, a nonlinear system is needed to reduce the size of the dataset.

Conclusion

Python is an excellent option for data retrieval, processing, and analysis. With so much data available and Python's advanced features, you can do almost anything you want. Who knows, maybe one day, once you've mastered data science and Python, you'll win an award for the algorithm you wrote in Python.

Hence, the future looks bright for data science, and Python is just a tiny portion of the pie. Thankfully, this book should give you a solid basis from which to go out and broaden your understanding of data science. Don't forget that if you put in the effort and time to learn Python Data Science, you could not only learn a new skill but also move up in your career.